The Farnsworth House

Haunting

On the Gettysburg Ghost Trail

Richard Estep

For my sister, Gwynn, with love.

Contents

Foreword

Everyone who knows me (or knows of me) has more than likely heard of my paranormal experiences in Gettysburg over the past 29 years, through television, books, and the Internet.

The ghost regiment I accidentally witnessed and filmed back in the summer of 1990, while on a family vacation, is probably the most well-known of them all; but another experience that happened during that same trip is not as well known, and frankly, I may have never mentioned it to anyone before.

Oddly enough, the location where it happened has probably been the focal point of many of my Gettysburg adventures throughout these years, in one way or another. Right there on Baltimore Street, just south of the center of town, sits one of Gettysburg's many colonial, red-brick homes turned bed and breakfast. But this is no ordinary house. The Farnsworth House can single-handedly paint a picture of the American tragedy that took place in July of 1863, right there on its doorstep.

It draws you in.

It beckons you to stare.

It dares you to enter.

So, there I was, a 17-year-old kid on a summer vacation with my mom and dad. One of our stops on that three-week trek was a few days in Gettysburg. I was such a history buff, and more specifically, I had a deep and unexplainable connection to the American Revolution and the Civil War. Maybe it was due to the fact I was from San Antonio, and battlegrounds were my backyard growing up. (Remember the Alamo? Sorry, I couldn't resist.)

Anyway, my parents and I stayed at the Holiday Inn (currently the 1863 Inn of Gettysburg) right next to the Jenny Wade House, at the convergence of Steinwehr and Baltimore. I made it just in time for the last tour of the day at the Jenny Wade House. She was the only civilian killed in the battle, as she was struck in the back by a stray bullet while in her kitchen baking bread for Union soldiers. I was enamored by the bullet holes still visible in the brick work of the small house. It really put into perspective how it must have been to be caught in the middle of a fire fight.

The tour guide mentioned that one of the theories on where the bullet that killed Jenny Wade came from, was that it had originated from the weapon of a sniper, firing from the attic of the Farnsworth House, just up the street about a quarter mile. I immediately made my way up Baltimore Street to check it out.

Desperation, panic, and urgency, are all feelings I got when I finally laid eyes on Farnsworth. The first thing you notice is the south wall of the house with its tiny, off-centered attic window at the top of a tall, solid brick side of the house. It is a perfect sniper position for the Confederacy, hovering over the front lines of the Union force, but it is also a wide-open position. Bullet holes riddle the south wall, and the feelings I mentioned are mainly due to the obvious pot shots Union soldiers were taking at the house, trying to hit the snipers in the tiny window.

Some shots were way off, and some were pretty close, but the muskets of those days had roughly the same distance accuracy of a stone throw. Whoever was in this attic, was shooting fish in a barrel down on the streets below, and nobody on the Union side was successful at taking them out.

I then made my way to the entrance. I was surprised that I could just walk into the house and wander around. Perhaps I wasn't supposed to, but back in 1990, they may not have been as organized a business as they are now.

I started up the stairs. As I rounded the corner, I noticed the arm, hips, and legs of a man sitting on the landing. The clothing was clearly dirty and ragged. His pants were almost of a burlap or cheap canvas quality, and his hands looked as filthy as an auto mechanic on a busy day.

My first inclination was that some period actor was taking a break. I had seen many of them around town. As I approached the landing, it was as if whatever I was looking at was a mirage. It just faded from sight as I got closer. I stepped back to my original position thinking that there was some optical illusion occurring, but all I saw was raw staircase.

That feeling of desperation came over me again. That heaviness is all over the town of Gettysburg, no matter where you go, but it is particularly strong in this house. It freaked me out a little, but curiosity pushed me further. I made it to the attic, and I crawled on my belly up to the window.

It was as if the modern town below suddenly vanished, and 1863 came into view in its place. I imagined what it must have looked like back then. I meditated on the reality that I was lying on the very same spot those snipers were. Hindsight is twenty-twenty, so I can attribute what happened next to a high-energy person plugging themselves into a high-energy environment. I got up, dusted myself off, and when I turned to leave, I suddenly found myself face-to-face with a man.

He was small, and probably in his twenties. He had that same ragged outfit that I had seen on the stairwell. His face had a large bushy mustache and was covered in grime. His hair was dark and disheveled. I noticed his striking green eyes. They have stuck with me to this day. Then there was the smell. He reeked of body odor, and gunpowder.

The apparition was there for a long enough time for all this to register with me, but just as quickly as I saw him, he was gone. The whole thing probably lasted two seconds, at best.

Two days later, I experienced the regiment at Pickett's Charge that I have become known for. I once again thought it was a group of reenactors, but they, too, disappeared from my sight. This time, I managed to get it on tape, and this is what really prompted me to research the paranormal.

My sighting at the Farnsworth House could have been written off as a figment of my imagination, but my VHS video recorder does not have an imagination. This was now my personal proof that these things existed.

In 2010, I was back in Gettysburg with my brother and our investigation team, filming the show *Ghost Lab* for the Discovery Channel. This was our Gettysburg episode, and it was a homecoming of sorts for me, because we visited the site of my Pickett's Charge experience. One of the places we investigated was the Jennie Wade House, and I had to do something to try and tie Farnsworth to it. So, we got three reenactors to dress up in Confederate garb with full weaponry, sit in the garret of the Farnsworth House, and then pretend to fire down on us while we were investigating the Jennie Wade House a little further up the street.

We created an environment of frantic chaos. We had speakers blaring, along with musket and cannon fire at both locations. We were running around telling everyone to take cover...

...and then it happened.

A loud female cry was heard by both my brother and I. It was also captured on our audio recording. Desperation, panic, and urgency were all in play once again, and not only was this tied to the activity at Farnsworth, it was also connected to the activity and emotion of the battle that still drifts through the streets of Gettysburg like a London fog.

Who was this little man at Farnsworth I saw in 1990?

How can an emotion be so powerful that even its putrid smell transcends space and time? These are all questions I constantly ask myself in all of my paranormal investigations, but especially every time I stand on the sidewalk outside the Farnsworth House all these years later, and stare at the poster child of a nation at war with itself.

— Brad Klinge

Introduction

Why Gettysburg?

It's a question that I am asked surprisingly often, whether it's during one of the interviews my publisher has me do in order to publicize an upcoming book release; for one of the TV shows I sometimes appear on; or simply by friends and co-workers, who are curious as to why I should spend a big chunk of my hard-earned vacation time going back to this small town in Pennsylvania, rather than chilling out on a tropical cruise, or some other do-nothing vacation.

Frankly, they have a point. To this day, I am hard-pressed to explain exactly what it is that draws me back to Gettysburg over and over again.

It is true that I have a deep and abiding interest in all things related to the American Civil War but there's more to it than that; after all, I don't find myself heading to Fredericksburg, Antietam, Harper's Ferry, or any of the other battlefields whose names are written in the pages of countless history books covering the period.

There is something about Gettysburg that exerts an indefinable but also undeniably strong pull, and I am far from the only person who seems to be susceptible to it. Numerous people have told me that they experience the same attraction. (Hopefully their spouses are as tolerant and understanding as mine).

It's a strange thing indeed for an Englishman born and bred to grow up with a fascination for the American Civil War, but I've had one for as long as I can remember.

Long before I first set foot in the United States back in 1989, I immersed myself in Civil War books and such documentaries as were available in the U.K. at the time; as with so many people, the monumental TV series *The Civil War* by master film-maker Ken Burns was instrumental in firing up my interest, as was the TV mini-series/movie *Gettysburg,* directed by Ron Maxwell. I became a huge fan of the latter, the running time of which was so long that it came on two VHS video tapes, and watched it over and over again.

Fast-forward more than a decade, and suddenly I find myself a Brit transplanted to America. I first visited Gettysburg in 2002. I was working as a computer networking engineer for IBM at the time, and they had sent me to the east coast in order to take a four-day class.

My manager was good enough to extend my flight

reservation by an extra day (thanks, Jim) and I resolved to make the best of it, dragging my less-than-thrilled wife at the time along with me on a road-trip to the crossroads town that loomed so large in my imagination.

Was it a disappointment to me? Not in the slightest. In fact, quite the contrary; as we walked through the streets, fields, and cemeteries, I found myself rapidly falling in love with the place. As my (now ex-) wife's mood grew increasingly sour, so mine became more and more buoyant (with hindsight, I should never have put her through the experience). Taking a bus tour of the battlefield with a qualified guide was, and still is, one of the best ways to get a feel for it all when you only have a short amount of time to spend there. Places that had only been names, and black-and-white photographs in books until that afternoon, suddenly became real to me. Pickett's Charge, Little Round Top, Devil's Den, and the Slaughter Pen, to name just a few, now held greater meaning for me than they ever had before, something that was only possible because I was finally walking the hallowed ground at Gettysburg.

As the sun began to set and the time to return to our hotel drew near, my wife felt like stopping off for a drink on the way back to the rental car. I couldn't deny that she had earned it, and so we stopped off at the first watering hole we came to — a place named, innocuously enough, the Farnsworth House Inn.

Stepping inside the tavern was like stepping back in time. Staff members dressed in period clothing, beautiful wooden furnishings, and best of all, a huge display case occupying an entire wall that contained memorabilia from the movie *Gettysburg,* all greeted us. I practically drooled as I took in every detail of the uniform worn by actor Jeff Daniels, in his iconic role as Joshua Lawrence Chamberlain, commander of the 20th Maine, and a host of other props and costumes. Only later would I find out that the Farnsworth House had served as the local pub for the majority of the *Gettysburg* cast and crew.

Wandering around the outside of the building, it felt as though the Farnsworth House practically *breathed* history. An informational sign told me that the building had been a Confederate redoubt during the battle, with sharpshooters occupying the attic; they had used its small garret window as a vantage point from which to snipe at the Union soldiers who were entrenched just up the road, on nearby Cemetery Hill.

I stood silently in front of one of the walls which faced

that very same hill, awe-struck by the more than 150 pock-marks in the brick, scars from where the Union soldiers had returned fire and vainly tried to eliminate the Confederates that had been harassing them for hours on end.

What must it have been like, I wondered, on those three hot days back in early July of 1863? Baltimore Street was fairly busy, with a steady stream of cars and pedestrians heading in both directions. Back then, the only thing going back and forth would have been bullets, as the Confederate and Union soldiers exchanged fire. Most of the town's citizens took shelter in their basements, waiting for the storm to pass them by.

Gettysburg is a peaceful town at night, particularly during the off-season, when most of the tourists have gone. Yet its many ghosts seem to be active all year round, and it is they which drew me back some fifteen years later. As a paranormal investigator and author of several books in that same field, I was just looking for a reason to come back to Gettysburg again, and this time, for more than just a day.

My lucky break came in the summer of 2017, when I was attending a Houston, Texas, paranormal convention, just a week or so after the city had been slammed with a major hurricane. Quite understandably, the con was poorly attended, to say the least, and those of us who had been invited to speak didn't have much else to do other than shoot the breeze with one another.

It was my good fortune to find myself sitting next to Brad and Barry Klinge, two Texas-based paranormal investigators who are perhaps best known for their work on the shows *Ghost Lab* and *Strange Curiosity*. The Klinge brothers both happened to be keen Civil War enthusiasts, and in between the occasional book signing, we talked about our favorite Civil War locations — and the ghosts that are said to haunt them.

Brad has been known to give a tour of Gettysburg on more than one occasion, taking visitors to some of the lesser-known parts of the battlefield. I had thought that I was well-versed in Gettysburg history and lore, but he went on to tell me story after story that I had never heard before. One of the most compelling was the so-called 'Battle of the Brickyard,' in which a Union brigade was brutally chewed up by a Confederate force more than twice its size. I resolved to visit the site of the battle, which was once known as Kuhn's Brickyard, myself, whenever I got the opportunity.

We also talked about the Farnsworth House. Brad and Barry had shot a segment there for the second season of

Ghost Lab. In it, they had tried to recreate the shot which had killed Jennie Wade, the only civilian to die during the Battle of Gettysburg; the bullet which killed her was believed by many to have been fired from the attic of the Farnsworth House, and the Klinges wanted to test the theory in a slightly more high-tech way. Unable to fire live bullets down the length of Baltimore Street, they instead substituted a laser beam. It was their hope that in doing so, they might stir up some paranormal activity as a consequence.

"You should check that place out," Brad told me, signing an autograph for a fan with a flourish. "It's a great mix of history and haunting."

I took his words to heart, but when I did get back to Gettysburg a few months later, I was focused on an entirely different location: the historic Fairfield Inn. The town of Fairfield was the scene of a little-known cavalry action on the third day of the battle. It is usually overshadowed by the momentous events taking place eight miles away during what has come to be known as Pickett's Charge, and rarely merits more than a mention in the history books, if that.

Built in 1757, the Fairfield Inn had its own reputation for being haunted, and it was a reputation that my team of paranormal investigators and I wanted to put to the test over the course of five days, when we took up residence at the inn and investigated the place for ourselves. (Readers who are interested in that particular case and location are referred to the book that covers it, *The Fairfield Haunting: On the Gettysburg Ghost Trail*).

Along the way, I got to walk the battlefield once more, and fell in love with it all over again. I was even able to stop off at the Farnsworth House for dinner and a drink or two at the end of the day, and just couldn't resist asking the bartenders and waitresses about the ghostly goings-on. They told me in no uncertain terms that the Farnsworth House was extremely active, paranormally speaking, and all of them had had multiple experiences and encounters during their time working there.

I spent the next six months working on other projects until, one day, I received an invitation to appear as a guest speaker at a charity event in Gettysburg during the summer of 2018. Organized by the good people at the Gettysburg Ghost Exchange, the Gettysburg Battlefield Bash is a three-day extravaganza that brings together paranormal enthusiasts and experts from across the country in order to benefit the Pennsylvania Wounded Warriors charity, among others.

How do you say no to such a worthy cause? I wasted no

time in accepting their invitation to speak, and then it hit me: I'd need someplace to lay my head while I was there. This might be just the opportunity I had been looking for...

When I explained that I would like to research and write a book about the haunting of their establishment, the powers that be at the Farnsworth House very graciously granted me permission to do so. We agreed that I would spend five days there, investigating overnight, attending the Battlefield Bash during three of the days, and sleeping whenever and wherever I could find the time.

I wanted the rooms with the most paranormal activity, or at the very least, those with the *reputation* for being the most haunted. My good friend and Gettysburg ghost expert Pam Barry had advised me to pick the McFarlane Room and the Sara Black Room. She had investigated them both before, and had gotten good results in both. Taking her at her word, I went ahead and reserved each room for two nights apiece.

Depending on the square footage of the location, I like to work with a team that is not only of a manageable size, but also has some skill and expertise in the field. For the Farnsworth investigation, I wanted to keep things relatively small and low-key, if for no other reason than to avoid disturbing the other paying guests at the inn.

Jason and Anna were both experienced investigators, having accompanied me to research many haunted locations over the years. I knew that I could trust them to do solid work, to function independently, and to keep a sense of humor when we all started to get tired and run-down, which I expected would happen in the final 72-96 hours when the lack of sleep really started to kick in.

Fortunately for me, they were more than eager to pack their equipment and jump on a plane with me, especially when they heard that we would be helping out a great charitable cause. Three seemed like an adequate number of people, so long as we investigated one single room at a time.

And just like that, it was done. We would have five days and four nights to research the haunting of the historic Farnsworth House Inn.

I could hardly wait to see what we uncovered.

Much like its predecessor, *The Fairfield Haunting*, this book is something of a strange beast, being neither entirely fish nor fowl. On the one hand, it is a book of ghost stories, all of them centered around the Battle of Gettysburg in general and the Farnsworth House Inn in particular. Some of these stories have resulted from interviews that I have conducted with the staff, guests, and visiting paranormal investigators. Others arose from entries written in the visitor's book.

When I recount these experiences, the reader should be aware that I am primarily fulfilling the role of storyteller, rather than that of an active paranormal investigator. Although I will attempt to offer explanations and alternative theories where possible, I have not experienced these things personally, and therefore cannot guarantee their accuracy or veracity to any great degree. Please understand that I am not disputing the honesty or the integrity of any of these eyewitnesses — but I simply wasn't there at the time they happened.

On the other hand, a significant section of the book details my own paranormal investigation at the Farnsworth House. During my four day stay, my team and I were fortunate enough to have access to two of the most haunted bedrooms, plus the garret, the cellar, and the dining room. While I must state from the outset that pots and pans weren't flying off the shelves during my stay, we did experience some phenomena that it is difficult to explain away in a conventional manner. This is not the kind of sensationalist book in which dark, malevolent entities lurk in every pool of shadow, but the Farnsworth House Inn most definitely has its ghosts, and I believe that some of them most definitely made their presence felt during the course of our stay. The reader will learn my reasons for making that claim as the book progresses.

While this is primarily a paranormal non-fiction book, it is my hope that it will sit just as comfortably in the Civil War history section of the library or bookstore. Leaving the ghosts aside for a moment, I wanted to take the reader along with me as I explored some of the more interesting sections of the battlefield. While those with an in-depth knowledge of the battle are unlikely to learn anything new here, many readers may find themselves learning a few things about the Gettysburg campaign that are entirely new to them.

Lastly, this book is something of a personal travel journal. My style of writing is such that I like to put the reader in the shoes of myself and my team-mates, walking the streets and fields of Gettysburg, prowling the rooms and hallways of the Farnsworth House, interviewing witnesses and searching for answers. As such, it contains a great deal of anecdote, subjectivity, and personal bias. Such is the nature of this particular beast.

So there you have it: the book you now hold in your

hands, are reading on the screen, or listening to in audio book form, is a paranormal-history-travel journal. If this isn't quite your cup of tea, I entirely understand.

Still with me? *Good!* Hopefully that means you're a part of my tribe, one of those fine people who has a passion for the Civil War and the phantoms that arose from it.

Let's hit the Gettysburg Ghost Trail and meet some of them, shall we?

Richard Estep
Longmont, Colorado
March 2019

Chapter One
A Haunted History

On July 1, 1863, the Army of the Potomac and the Army of Northern Virginia, two vast military forces that had been playing a game of cat and mouse with one another, finally locked horns to the north and west of a small town in Pennsylvania.

Forced onto the defensive, the Union army retreats, its faltering units pushed back toward the town of Gettysburg in some disarray. Along with the soldiers come a number of civilians, who have been unfortunate enough to find themselves placed directly in the path of the conflict.

There are so many wounded Union soldiers that, by late afternoon, it becomes necessary for the Union army to commandeer many of the public and private buildings to act as makeshift hospitals.

Two families — the Slentzes and the Weikerts — ride out the entirety of the battle at a two-and-a-half story residence known as the Sweney House. The Weikerts are already there, lodgers of the owner, Harvey Sweney, whereas the Slentzes are refugees from west of town. Union soldiers (both wounded and not) fill the Sweney House on day one of the battle, sleeping there, eating there, and getting their wounds patched up.

The damaged but not yet defeated Union army concentrates its forces upon Cemetery Hill and the area around it, creating a stronghold on which to anchor its defensive line. While this is being done, townsfolk of Gettysburg are warned to go down into their cellars and stay there until the fighting has stopped.

Confederates have now chased the last remnants of the Union army clear through the town, going from house to house, either taking the Union soldiers prisoner, or in some cases, killing them where they are found. By nightfall on the first day, the Sweney House and all of those around it are in Rebel hands. The closest Union position is to be found on Cemetery Hill.

For the next two days, the two sides have at one another. Opposing lines of skirmishers slug it out in the no man's land separating Cemetery Hill and the southern edge of town, trading shots with one another, but making no real headway in either direction. These skirmishers are the type of men who have taken up temporary residence in the

Sweney House.

It is impossible to say for sure which specific units occupy the Sweney House at any given moment, as the situation is both fluid and confused, primarily due to the fog of war. The attics of most houses on the south end of town are occupied by sharpshooters, many of whom take great delight in punching out firing holes in the walls, and then harassing the enemy with sporadic fire.

Rather than brave the storm of lead outside in the street, some soldiers breach the walls that separate one house from another, so that they can run the entire length of a block without running the risk of getting their heads blown off.

Window panes are shattered. The wooden and brick walls are riddled with bullet holes. Citizens huddle together by lantern-light in their cellars, as their homes are shot to pieces above their heads. Countless thousands of rounds are exchanged over the course of those two days.

The fighting slackens on the afternoon of July 3rd, as the momentous events of Pickett's Charge take place. That night, when it becomes obvious that Lee's last gasp attack has failed, the Confederates slowly withdraw their forces from the town. The following morning, the 4th of July (Saturday) the Sweney House and the rest of Gettysburg are back in Union hands once more.

Harvey Sweney, erstwhile owner of the house, dies in 1870. The house passes to his daughter, Elizabeth Sweney, who, in turn, sells it to her mother, Catherine (something which would have most likely displeased Harvey to no end). She lives there until her death in 1908.

The following year, a local family — the Blacks — take ownership of the house, converting it into a place of lodging that caters to the many visitors who flock to Gettysburg each year. 'Sleepy Hollow Lodge,' as it is called, sees thousands of guests pass through its doors over the course of the next four decades, and becomes a popular fixture on the Gettysburg tourist map.

The Blacks — George and Verna — bequeath the house to their daughter, Sara, and it remains in the family until 1972, when it is sold to a couple named Loring and Jean Shultz, who are also local to Gettysburg. The house needs a little work, and so the Shultzes invest a great deal of money into restoring the place to its former glory, and also adding a first-rate restaurant for good measure.

At the time of writing (the spring of 2019) the Farnsworth House remains high on the list of must-see locations at Gettysburg. Many come for good beer and fine dining, and to see the large collection of *Gettysburg* movie memorabilia that is on display in the tavern. Others come because of the building's unique place in history, its role in Gettysburg lore well-known around the world.

And others…others are drawn there because of the ghosts.

During almost twenty-five years spent investigating haunted houses on both sides of the Atlantic, it has been my experience that places such as the Farnsworth House seem to 'find their people.' By this, I mean that some people appear to be inexorably drawn to those places somehow. It is almost as if the haunted houses have a knack of finding the right person for the right place.

One such person is Kayla, who takes great satisfaction in her job as a tour guide at the Farnsworth House. She plainly has a deep and abiding affection for the place, and during my visit she turned out to be an absolutely invaluable treasure trove of information concerning the house, its hauntings, and the remarkable events that engulfed it in the summer of 1863.

When I first met Kayla, in the summer of 2018, she had

been conducting ghost tours in Gettysburg for some fourteen years. There weren't many questions that she wasn't able to answer right away.

Kayla had almost lost count of the strange occurrences that she had either witnessed or experienced personally at the Farnsworth House. One of the most memorable took place in the Jennie Wade room, which is not part of the main house; rather, it is a newer addition that is located outside.

She admittedly found the room to be a little creepy when she first set foot inside, but then, what else was one to expect from a place with a haunted reputation as great as that of the Farnsworth? During their stay in that room, Kayla's husband took great delight in making fun of her, laughing and calling her a 'big chicken.'

The atmosphere was freaking her out a little, but despite that, Kayla finally managed to fall asleep. She awoke with a start in the dead of night, sitting bolt upright in bed. Looking at the bedside alarm clock, she saw that it was almost four o'clock in the morning.

It took a moment for her to fully wake up and realize just what it was that had disturbed her: the sound of footsteps, loud and heavy, stomping on the floor up above her. "It sounded like they were having a polka party up there," she laughs, before adding that she was starting to get a little upset, as she had to be up at eight o'clock for breakfast. How dare the occupants of the room above be so inconsiderate as to be dancing around at that unearthly time of the morning?

She called out in annoyance, yelling at the inconsiderate guests to stop.

"They're not gonna hear you," her husband mumbled sleepily.

Nor did they. The footsteps continued unabated for the next hour. Breathing a sigh of relief, Kayla finally went back to sleep, snatching a couple more precious hours before daybreak.

Eight o'clock came around all too quickly. Before sitting down to eat breakfast, she stopped by the front desk to turn in her key.

"How was your stay?" the house representative asked her cheerfully.

"Great, except for the people stomping around upstairs, having their own little party this morning," she replied.

"Honey, what room were you in?"

Kayla told her that she had been staying in the Jennie Wade room. Instantly, the representative grew still. "There's no room above you," she said quietly.

That would be just the first of numerous encounters Kayla would have with the ghosts of the Farnsworth House, and after spending several years working there and interacting with the spirits on a semi-regular basis, she still manages to find out something new about them every once in a while. They are, by all accounts, a diverse and fascinating bunch.

Take, for example, the spirit of Jeremy, a young boy who was supposedly killed during an accident in the street outside, when he was run over by a horse-drawn carriage or buggy. The story goes that Jeremy's broken body was brought inside the Farnsworth House in order to receive medical attention, but all efforts to save the poor young fellow were in vain, and he passed away in what is now the bathroom of the Sara Black room...which I would spend two nights sleeping in during my stay at the house. (Jeremy's father, heartbroken at the loss of his son, has also been seen and sensed at the Farnsworth — usually in the McFarlane room, which would also be my bedroom for two nights).

An equally sad tale is that of a young lady named Florence, who is believed to have died after tragically giving birth to a still-born child. Her spirit is said to haunt the building to this day, as is that of her midwife.

Another Farnsworth House spirit goes by the name of Mary. The story goes that she was either a nurse or a medical assistant, and she seems to enjoy taking care of the guests and residents of the Farnsworth House long after her death.

Jeremy is not the only mischievous young boy ghost to run and play throughout the house. He is sometimes accompanied by a phantom playmate named Billy. The pair likes to play games and practical jokes on unsuspecting staff and guests, whenever the opportunity arises.

A girl named Cecilia, who died of respiratory failure when she was very young, has also made her presence felt at the Farnsworth. According to the psychic medium who last encountered her, Cecilia has long, curly blonde hair, and wears an old-fashioned ankle-length dress.

It must be emphasized that much of the available information about the spirits of the Farnsworth comes from mediums such as this, and should therefore be taken with a grain of salt; accurate and detailed historical records for every visitor and resident of the house do not exist, and as such, many of these stories are difficult, if not impossible, to verify.

What *can* be said, however, is that there is a long and very solid track record of paranormal phenomena taking place at the Farnsworth House that tracks with the personalities and supposed identities of some of these spirits; Jeremy, for example, is a name that has cropped up on spirit boxes and EVPs on multiple occasions, and he seems to respond well when presented with toys and other similar gifts.

During my investigation at the Farnsworth, one of my objectives was to see if my team and I could gather evidence to support the existence of these entities.

It would prove to be a fascinating journey.

Chapter Two

First Night

When I opened the door to the McFarlane Room and stepped inside, my first thought was simply: "*Wow*."

To say that the room looked a little *creepy* would be an understatement. The only thing missing from the Victorian-style bedroom was the figure of Ebenezer Scrooge sitting in the wooden rocking chair next to the ornate four-poster bed. The scene was positively Dickensian; with the exception of a small TV screen and a swamp cooler to oppose the humid August heat, the room looked as though it had been frozen in time sometime during the mid-19th century.

The room was a little on the small side compared to modern hotel rooms, which was very much in keeping with the historic nature of the building. A painting of Confederate General Robert E. Lee adorned the wall closest to the windows facing the street, while the other walls were decorated with a large mirror, and a set of child's clothing that came from the same period. A compact *en suite* bathroom hosted a lovely old claw-footed bathtub.

Every residential room at the Farnsworth House Inn is named after a person or persons who have played a significant role in its past history. John Findly McFarlane was one such man. Prominent locally and politically-connected, he (along with Martha, his wife) was the original owner and builder of the house, constructing it in 1833 for the princely sum of $700 — a small fortune back then.

Despite having been an enterprising man of means, John McFarlane was not necessarily a lucky man; the bank stripped him of his assets in 1842, in what appears to have been something akin to a bankruptcy. The Farnsworth House was one of those assets. Yet even though the McFarlanes owned the house for just ten years, their name and legacy lives on in the name of the room that I was to call home for the next two nights.

It had been a long day. My fellow investigators, Jason and Anna, were every bit as tired as I was, so we didn't have much in the way of research planned for that first night. We agreed that it would be a good idea for us to call it an early night, and hit the ground running the next day. They were both staying off-site at a hotel. Figuring that immersion might be the best way to elicit some kind of response, I had elected to spend the night alone in the McFarlane Room.

After showering and brushing my teeth, I pulled back the covers and settled down with my tablet to take a few notes before bedtime. The four-poster was surprisingly comfortable, and after flipping through a few reviews for the Farnsworth House on TripAdvisor, I turned out all but the dimmest light in order to get some sleep.

One of the stories that frequently came up was that of a mournful male apparition, who was sometimes seen sitting in the rocking chair at the side of the bed. Visiting mediums had claimed that this was the father of Jeremy; the playful little boy was also believed to haunt the room himself, along with the spirit of a Confederate sergeant, one of the sharpshooters who had been stationed up in the attic. As I rolled onto my side and drifted off to sleep, my last thought was that hopefully at least one of them would pay me a visit during the night.

Something dragged me from my sleep; something loud and metallic-sounding. I sat up, looking around in the darkness of the room. The eerie-looking child's clothing gave me a bit of a start, but nothing seemed out of place. I looked at my watch: it was a little after three o'clock in the morning.

The noise came again. I soon figured out that it was coming from the water pipes, which made a clanking, clattering sound for no apparent reason. That was an easy debunk: old building, old plumbing. I suspected that some of the guests who had reported unexplained loud banging sounds in the night might have heard the same thing and misinterpreted it as being paranormal. It would be an easy thing to do after dark, particularly if you were half-asleep and already a little uneasy because of the room's reputation.

The pipes continued to wake me up throughout the night at roughly quarter-hour intervals. At around four o'clock, there came a loud pounding from the hallway outside my room. *That* was no water pipe. Grabbing the room key, I opened the door and went out onto the landing. More thuds, this time from the foot of the stairs. I went down and opened the front door, only to be faced with two *very* intoxicated guests. Apologetically, they explained that they had slipped out for an early-morning smoke and had forgotten to bring their room key with them. I let them back in and asked whether anything unusual had happened to them during their stay; sadly, the only spirits they had encountered had come straight out of a bottle.

I slept undisturbed for the rest of the night. A number of

coins that I had scattered around the room to be used as control objects were still exactly how I had left them.

So far, my first night at the Farnsworth House had yielded no ghostly activity at all. I had slept relatively soundly – unlike some of the room's other visitors, who had gotten a little more than they bargained for.

Chapter Three

The Face at the Door

Joe Natalini is not a man given to flights of fancy. As a police officer, he is, by necessity, something of a pragmatist. This is a fairly common trait among the men and women in blue who protect our society. They tend to be rational, logical thinkers, not to mention trained observers, and can quite often be very skeptical, which is quite understandable when one considers the fact that they are used to being lied to on a daily basis.

These were just some of the reasons why I found Joe to be such a credible witness when I interviewed him on the subject of the ghostly encounter that he and his wife had at the Farnsworth House. We sat down together at the Gettysburg Battlefield Bash. In a measured, methodical manner, Joe laid out the timeline of strange events that had happened to them in the McFarlane room.

The Natalinis were staying overnight, attending an organized public ghost hunt. The group was enthusiastic after having heard a number of disembodied knocks and then recorded several EVPs down in the cellar. At 3:30 in the morning, things were starting to wind down. Joe and his wife retired to their room for the night.

Although he and the rest of his group had set out to focus on investigating the attic and the cellar, Joe had also wanted to make sure that he had covered all of his bases. This was why, at around 7:30 the previous evening, he had set up a trail-cam in the McFarlane room. He had carefully positioned the unit next to the TV, with its lens and motion sensor facing the bed. The camera covered most of the room, and should be triggered if anything moved in there. Satisfied that he had placed the trail-cam correctly, Joe had locked the door, and gone out to enjoy the evening's ghost hunt.

The camera was set to video mode, rather than single shot. When he and his wife returned to the room a few hours before sunrise, they washed up and climbed into bed. Joe's wife, Michelle, was asleep as soon as her head hit the pillow, but sleep eluded him. The law enforcement officer was still amped up from the ghost hunt.

He tried to relax by watching a little television. There wasn't anything interesting on at that time of the morning, and Joe soon found himself zoning out...until, that is, he noticed something standing at the foot of the bed.

He blinked, unable to believe what he was seeing. Surely, his eyes *had* to be playing tricks on him…weren't they? Because there, not eight away from Joe, stood the unmistakable form of a black shadow figure.

The thing was at least six feet tall, its features so indistinct that he could not tell whether it was a male or a female — but it definitely had arms, legs, a torso, and a head, and if he had been a betting man, Joe would have said that it had the physique of a man. As a police officer, Joe was well-used to picking out details on potential suspects, even in low-light conditions. This was the last thing he had ever expected to find standing at the foot of his bed.

Before going to bed, he had left the door to the room cracked ever so slightly ajar, allowing a little ambient light from the hallway outside to enter. As he watched with mounting disbelief, the figure began to move in the direction of the doorway, blotting out the light coming around the doorframe for a second, and then just disappeared.

Joe turned to his wife, and shook her awake. As she opened her eyes groggily, he told her what he had just witnessed.

"Honey, are you sure you weren't sleeping?" she asked.

"No, I am *wide* awake!"

Taking him at his word, she pulled the covers up and over her head, and snuggled up closer to her husband. Whatever this mysterious shadow figure was, or represented, she wanted absolutely *nothing* to do with it.

There was no way that Joe was going to sleep now. He had a feeling that the McFarlane Room wasn't done with him yet. As things turned out, he was absolutely right.

The black, amorphous mass was difficult to see at first. About the same size as a basketball, it appeared to be floating in mid-air, roughly halfway up the wall. Joe stared at it in complete silence, watching the anomaly rise upward, make a right-hand turn, and then disappear into the ceiling.

That wasn't all. Joe's gaze was drawn toward the door. Something out in the hallway had caught his attention.

It was a face.

Somebody was looking in at him through the space in the door frame.

It wasn't a shadow figure this time. On the contrary, what looked back at Joe from outside his room had a clearly-discernible eye, nose, mouth, and other facial features. This was undoubtedly the face of a man.

At first, Joe thought that it might have been a fellow guest of the Farnsworth House…until he realized that he had seen everybody else who was part of the ghost-hunting event, and this didn't look like any of them. Nor had they made a single, solitary sound. The floorboards outside the McFarlane Room are, like the rest of the original structure, old and well-used, which made them extremely creaky. The same could also be said of the staircase which lies to the right of the doorway. It would be nigh-on impossible for somebody to sneak up to that door without making at least a little bit of noise.

Who the hell is looking in through my door?!?

Joe leapt out of bed and made straight for the doorway, his eyes never leaving it, not even for a split-second. The mysterious peeper darted to the right, making for the staircase that leads down and out to the street.

Flinging the door wide open, Joe went out onto the landing at the top of the stairs…

…which were completely deserted.

His cop brain started working overtime, calculating potential solutions to explain what had just happened. Every single time, he came up short. There was no rational explanation. There was just no way for the person he had confronted to have been a living, breathing human being. It simply wasn't possible.

Joe woke Michelle up once again, and explained that he was at the end of his rope. "I need to get some sleep," he told her, "and there's no way I'll be able to do that with all this going on. Let's pack up our stuff and get out."

Which is exactly what they did.

"I don't minding hunting it, or finding it," Joe reflects, with the benefit of hindsight, "but when it's time for me to go to sleep, well…let's just say that I don't need *them* hunting *me*."

Few, I suspect, would disagree with him on that.

The drive home took the better part of two hours. Joe had never been so happy to slip into his own familiar, comfortable bed in all his life. After sleeping for a few hours, he woke up with the urge to see what his trail-cam might have picked up the night before.

What he found there shocked him beyond all belief.

The camera had been tripped twice. The first time was easily explainable, being nothing more than Michelle coming into the room in order to get a few things. The second, however, was something else entirely.

Staring intently at the computer screen, Joe watched as a dark shape appeared on the right-hand side of the room (opposite the windows). He had left the bedside night light on to provide a little ambient illumination for the camera to see by. The dark shape — whatever it was — passed directly in front of the night light, blocking it out for a split second, moving from right to left. This meant that the thing had to pass *through* the bed, before disappearing on the other side of the room.

As if that wasn't enough, the trail-cam itself could then be seen to shake, as though something had given it a hefty whack and knocked it off-balance…either that, or physically picked the camera up and moved it.

When we met to conduct our interview in person, I asked that Joe please bring the footage along with him for me to take a look at. I tend to be given a great number of photographs and video clips each year, from colleagues, clients, and readers, most of whom are acting in good faith. The vast majority tend to be easily debunkable, usually turning out to be reflected light, dust particles, insects, and other similarly mundane things.

This, I realized after viewing it for the first time, was something entirely different. Although it's impossible to say for sure, even after using video enhancement techniques and scrutinizing the footage frame by frame, I feel confident in saying that the dark shape moves in a manner consistent with a human being walking — which begs the question: just how, exactly, could a person walk *through* a bed?

Then there is the bigger picture to be considered. When Michelle had entered the room earlier, the door had been opened. The camera's field of vision had been able to pick that up. Yet when the mysterious nocturnal visitor made their appearance, the door had *not* opened — which meant that either somebody had entered Joe and Michelle's room without permission earlier that day (prior to them setting up the trail camera) and hid out there, out of sight, for *hours* upon end…or the McFarlane Room had been visited by some kind of entity while they were out.

At a loss for a rational (i.e. non-paranormal) explanation, Joe passed the footage on to some of his fellow police officers. This is a group of men and women who possess finely-tuned, inbuilt 'bullshit detectors,' for lack of a better term — that's a side-effect of being lied to for a living. You tend to look at an anomaly from all possible angles before rushing to judgment on something like this.

The camera was set up at around 6:30 PM at night, and was triggered at 11:30, some five hours later. None of the cops were buying into the idea of a highly-disciplined prankster lurking in the room after all that time, just as Joe hadn't bought into it either. Perhaps a member of staff was responsible, one with a master pass-key? How, then, can we explain the door not being opened at any point after Michelle had returned the room?

The only logical explanation to fit all the facts was the paranormal one. As we wrapped up our interview and shook hands, I found myself wondering whether the dark entity would decide to pay me a visit that coming night.

Chapter Four

"It Sounds Like Whispering"

Having heard through the magic of social media that a lady named Lisa had had quite the frightening experience at the Farnsworth House, I was intrigued, and wanted to learn more about it. When I reached out to her, she was more than happy to tell me her extraordinary story.

She had spent the night in the McFarlane Room, along with her best friend, Nikki. The ladies checked in at five o'clock in the afternoon, left their bags in the room, and then went out to first get some food, before taking in some of the sights of Gettysburg.

Being paranormal enthusiasts, Lisa and Nikki were interested in one thing above all others: ghosts. Rather than take a guided tour, however, they had wanted to check out some of the less well-known places in the area. Many would-be ghost hunters flock to Sachs Covered Bridge (my very limited experience there was written about in *The Fairfield Haunting: On the Gettysburg Ghost Trail*). Yet Gettysburg has a second bridge that also has a reputation for being haunted.

Although its proper name is the John Eisenhower Bridge, it has somehow earned itself the nickname of 'Suicide Bridge.' Built in 1886, some 23 years after the Battle of Gettysburg, the bridge spans Willoughby Run. The bridge has no particular reason to be haunted that I am aware of, and yet that has not prevented it from attaining a certain notoriety and mystique among paranormal enthusiasts.

It was dark by the time the ladies had finished their dinner and driven out toward the bridge. They turned slowly onto Waterworks Road, and drove carefully, the headlights of their car lighting up the trees, bushes, and fields along the side of the road.

A cyclist suddenly emerged from the darkness. His bicycle had no lights, and he was rather foolishly wearing no reflective gear. One moment the road was empty, the next, there he was, illuminated in the car headlights.

Seemingly oblivious to the vehicle coming up behind him, the cyclist swerved in front of them, moving from the right-hand side of the road to the left. Nikki slammed her foot down on the brakes, terrified that she might hit him.

They overtook the man slowly. Nikki watched in her side mirror as he stopped at the side of the road and stared at them. Pulling over, she slipped the car into park. Something about the man's appearance didn't seem right to her. He was old, with a long, grey beard, and, in Nikki's own words, he "looked creepy…*Hills Have Eyes* creepy…"

In most stereotypical Gettysburg ghost stories, we would expect such a man to be wearing period clothing; in fact, his manner of dress was very contemporary, including a pair of shorts that barely covered his spindly, stick-thin white legs.

"What's he doing?" Lisa asked, turning her head to try and get a better look.

"He just got off his bike," Nikki told her, watching in the side-mirror. The old man was glaring at them, his gaze practically shooting daggers. "He's just…staring at us…and he does *not* look happy. Take a look at the backup camera."

She reached out and flipped on the rear-mounted camera, which was used to make reversing the car a safer process.

"He's not back there," Lisa said, squinting. "There's nobody there."

"Yes there is — I can see him in the mirror with my own eyes!"

The old man was visible with the naked eye, but wasn't showing up on the camera, which was showing the rest of the road with a reasonable degree of detail, thanks to the red glow of the brake lights.

Then, just like that, he was gone.

Frowning, Nikki put the car into reverse gear and backed up to where she had last seen him. There was nowhere the old man could have gone, and yet, he had seemingly vanished into thin air, right before their disbelieving eyes.

This frightening experience spooked both ladies so much that they decided to cut short their excursion to Suicide Bridge, and head on back to the Farnsworth House.

If they were expecting a quiet night in the McFarlane Room, however, they would soon realize that they were out of luck.

After washing up for the night and climbing into bed, they lay there in the semi-darkness, just talking about this and that. They had made a point of switching off the air conditioning first, in order to cut out a major source of potential noise contamination.

The atmosphere was a little creepy — par for the course in the McFarlane Room after dark, as I can personally attest — but nothing particularly strange was going on.

"If there's somebody in here with us, please knock twice," Lisa said, not really expecting an answer.

The loud bang which emanated from the closet made

both women jump.

Then, right on the heels of the first one, there came a second bang, seeming to originate from the very same place.

They took out their phones and began snapping pictures, focusing on the area at the foot of the bed. After firing off a few bursts, Lisa started flipping back through her photos. Nothing. Nothing. Nothing…and then, a strange white mist, seemingly hovering in front of the closet.

Despite their best efforts to initiate further communication, requesting more knocks and physical signs to help prove that an unseen someone or something was in the room with them, everything remained quiet. Finally, they switched out the bedside light, rolled over, and tried to get some sleep.

That's when the noises started.

At first, they were relatively easy to explain. Pings and pops coming from the radiator could be easily explained away by the device flexing and contracting, a very common and entirely natural occurrence — under normal circumstances, at least. But this was the summertime, and the radiator hadn't been switched on in months. It was stone cold to the touch.

After that came the footsteps, walking back and forth

along the landing outside their room. The noises came at intermittent intervals, and just when Lisa and Nikki were drifting off to sleep once more, they started up again. It seemed almost calculated, as though somebody didn't want them to get any sleep that night.

Finally, they managed to fall asleep again. Although she couldn't tell exactly how much time had passed, Nikki was woken up again, what felt like just a short while later, by the sound of whispering. It was coming from somewhere inside the room with them.

Perhaps, she thought, it might be Lisa, talking in her sleep. Lisa's back was to her, and although the sound didn't seem to be coming from her direction — it also seemed to be farther away — some old buildings have strange acoustic properties, and the mind is also more than capable of playing tricks in the dark.

"Lisa," she hissed. "Are you awake?"

"Yeah."

"Do you hear that?"

"Yeah. It sounds like whispering."

The voices were indistinct, but it sounded very much as if there were two of them, carrying on a conversation. Both women were adamant that this wasn't simply the sound of somebody in a nearby room carrying on a conversation — this was coming from inside the McFarlane Room. Nikki believed it originated from the rocking chair, the same chair in which the apparition of Jeremy's distraught father is sometimes said to appear.

The phenomena then graduated from noises to physical touching. Nikki's hair began to be pulled, tugged on from behind. The only thing behind her was the empty rocking chair.

Without the air conditioning running, the room soon began to get hot and stuffy. Laying on her right side, Lisa started to feel cold chills running up and down her left side. It was as if one hemisphere of her body was in the freezer, while the other half was in the oven.

Utterly exhausted after a long, mostly sleepless night, they finally fell asleep at around five o'clock in the morning, just as the sky was beginning to lighten outside. At two minutes to seven, Nikki shook Lisa awake.

"Lisa, when did you get out of bed?"

"Huh?" Lisa asked blearily, still half-asleep. "What are you talking about? I never got out of bed."

"Then who did THAT?" Nikki demanded, pointing toward the bottom of the bed. Lisa sat up to get a better look.

The duvet, which had covered them both throughout the early part of the night (there's no better security blanket in a haunted room!) had been neatly folded across the foot of the bed. It had even been tucked underneath the mattress on both sides, as a chambermaid or member of the housekeeping staff might have done. Although they had pushed the duvet down earlier that morning, when the room had gotten a little too warm for their comfort, they had scrunched it down with their feet...what they were looking at now, on the other hand, would have satisfied even the most demanding drill sergeant at boot camp. It was stretched so taut, you could have bounced a quarter off it.

That was the final straw. The ladies packed their bags and left.

When I spoke with them, a few weeks after their visit, they had gotten past the fear that their brush with the paranormal had caused, and were now completely intrigued by the mysteries that they had been exposed to; in fact, they had already booked in for a return visit. This time, they were going to spend a night in the Sara Black Room.

I could only wonder if they would sleep peacefully or not – especially as I would soon be moving into that room myself.

Chapter Five

The Shadow Returns

I was sitting at my author's table at the Gettysburg Battlefield Bash, signing a few books, people-watching, and talking to passers-by, when a very nice couple approached me and said hello. They introduced themselves as Anthony and Deena. They had experienced something strange at the Farnsworth House, they said, and wanted to share it with me.

Shaking their hands, I invited them to sit down, then took out my voice recorder and began an impromptu interview.

They had stayed at the Farnsworth House for a couple of days the summer before, not long after the 4th of July weekend — the anniversary of the Battle of Gettysburg.

Anthony and Deena were both well aware of the Farnsworth's reputation for being haunted, but didn't think too much of it when they checked into the McFarlane Room on their first day. They had an interest in paranormal research, and the idea of sleeping in an active room appealed to them.

After unpacking their things, they took a moment to leaf through the guestbook, combing through the written experiences of previous guests. One of the things that stood out to them both were those accounts which claimed that the exterior wall — the one facing the street — always set off EMF meters.

"All I had to do to debunk that, was to look outside the window," Anthony chuckled. "The utility lines run right by that wall. No wonder their equipment was going off!"

Later that night, they took it in turns to wash up and clean their teeth before going to bed. Deena went first. When Anthony emerged, closing the bathroom door behind him, they both heard a colossal BOOM come from inside there.

Reasoning that something must have fallen, he re-traced his steps and went back inside. Everything was in place. He could see no explanation whatsoever for the extremely loud bang, which both of them had heard very clearly. The phenomenon defied their very best efforts to debunk it.

Their hopes that this might be the start of a paranormally-active night proved unfounded, however. All remained peaceful, allowing Anthony and Deena a good night's sleep. The following day was a busy, fun-packed one, which saw them exploring Gettysburg and the surrounding area. They spent a second restful night sleeping in the same room, and must have begun to wonder whether the Farnsworth House truly deserved its haunted reputation.

When they went to breakfast the following morning, things took a definite turn for the bizarre. They had left video cameras running inside the McFarlane Room, along with a few EMF meters and other sensing devices…just in case.

Everything seemed perfectly normal when they returned to the room, Anthony and Deena switched off their equipment, packed their bags, and went home.

Then came the evidence review.

Anthony sat in front of the monitor, watching the video footage spool by. Paranormal investigators are used to doing this, the most onerous task imaginable, for hours on end, often with nothing to show for it; in this case, however, they managed to hit the jackpot right away.

Just five minutes after they had closed the door behind them, every EMF sensor in the room went off, maxing out into the red zone. It would take a significant spike in electromagnetic energy to achieve such an effect, something far more powerful than somebody in an adjoining room making a phone call or sending a text.

While this isn't something that we can label as being definitively paranormal, it is certainly interesting — particularly when seen in the context of what happened next.

Hardly able to believe what he was seeing, Anthony watched as a large black shadow moved across the camera's field of view. He ran the footage back and played it again, frowning. There was nothing visible within the room that could have accounted for the strange effect. The windows were covered, and nothing inside there was capable of moving by itself.

As they told their story, I sat back in my chair, lost in thought. This was now the second person in as many days that had captured video evidence of a mysterious, moving shadow in the McFarlane Room. Others had reported seeing it with their own eyes. Taken as a whole, this made for some pretty compelling eyewitness testimony, I thought.

Purely by chance, Anthony and Deena had set up their camera in almost exactly the same spot that Joe had positioned his: directly facing the bed. Both had captured an inexplicable, shadowy anomaly in a closed and locked room, without any exterior sources of light or shadow. The similarities were remarkable…and more than a little creepy. The only difference was that in their video, the shadow moved from left to right — in the opposite direction to that captured by Joe.

Yet again, the McFarlane Room had delivered. Now I was *really* looking forward to spending another night in there.

Chapter Six

The Attic

The Farnsworth House attic — or *garret*, as it is also known — is not nearly as cramped and claustrophobic as one might think. Nevertheless, it's not exactly spacious (many adults would most likely hit their head on the ceiling if they were standing up straight) and I found it hard to imagine the fighting and living conditions that the Confederate soldiers stationed there had been forced to deal with. These sharp shooters kept up a steady stream of harassing fire along the length of Baltimore Street, picking targets of opportunity on Cemetery Hill, which had quickly become a key Union stronghold on the first day of the battle.

As was mentioned earlier, some historians believe that it was from this location, through the single, tiny garret window facing Cemetery Hill, that one of the Confederate sharp shooters accidentally shot Virginia 'Jennie' Wade, the only civilian to be killed during the battle. While most of the residents of Gettysburg had taken shelter in their cellars, this brave young woman was hard at work in her kitchen, baking bread for the Union soldiers that had been wounded while fighting to defend the hill.

It would have been a freak, one-in-a-million shot. The Confederate soldiers were not deliberately targeting civilians — Jennie was simply unlucky, and sadly she paid the ultimate price for her act of kindness, dying on the floor of what is now known as the Jennie Wade House. It is doubtful whether the soldier who fired the fateful shot ever found out that he had killed an innocent civilian by mistake.

"You'll want to keep an eye out for Walter up here," Kayla had told us.

"Who's Walter?"

"It's believed that Walter is the name of the man who accidentally shot Jennie Wade. He's still in residence here."

If that was true, then the reason for his spirit still being present at the Farnsworth House some 155 years after the Battle of Gettysburg would have to be a compelling one. While some have theorized that Walter is earthbound due to the massive guilt that would come along with accidentally shooting a non-combatant, if he didn't actually *know* that he was culpable, then there would be no reason for guilt. Combat is a confusing and tempestuous experience even at the best of times, and the maelstrom of a firefight raging in between the Farnsworth House and Cemetery Hill was most certainly not the best of times for those involved. The Confederate sharpshooters would have been too busy aiming, firing, and reloading, to notice where a stray bullet ended up — and could not possibly have seen Jennie Wade fall anyway, as she was hit while standing inside a house.

While I had to wonder whether 'Walter' truly existed, I was aware that there were at least some anecdotal reports to support the presence of Confederate spirits up there in the garret. In fact, stories of phantom Confederate sharp-shooters haunting the attic of the Farnsworth House go back for many years. It is not uncommon for guests to report hearing the thudding of boots on the ceiling above them, accompanied by the sound of heavy objects being dragged across the attic floor. Indeed, these auditory phenomena are not unique to the Farnsworth House; a number of Gettysburg residents have reported hearing the same thing in their own homes and business, reflecting the fact that soldiers often took up position in attics, firing down on their enemies from above.

During an episode of the TV show *Ghost Hunters*, which shot a segment at the Farnsworth House, TAPS members Jason Hawes and Steve Gonsalves spent some time in the attic themselves. While Jason claims to hear what sounds like a voice in his ear, he accepts that it may have been Steve's stomach growling (which Steve himself denies). This is followed by an indistinct sound, which the two men thought sounded like a male voice. Unfortunately, it's impossible to tell whether this was the sound of somebody else inside the house speaking, or a voice coming from somewhere outside in the street — we would learn during our investigation of the attic that noise contamination from both of these sources was a fairly frequent problem.

The present-day owners of the Farnsworth House have gated the garret window off from the rest of the attic, in order to protect the delicate frame and the glass within it. This does not seem to have reduced the number of ghostly encounters that continue to take place there.

As we climbed the staircase leading up to the attic, I should really have been paying more attention. I was lost in my own thoughts, trying to imagine what it must have been like for those gray-jacketed soldiers in the summer of 1863. The house was full of smoke, a by-product of the steady stream of rifle-fire emanating from the windows.

The doorway leading into the attic has a fairly low frame. I found this out the hard way, when the top of my head slammed into it with enough force to make me see stars.

"Are you okay, man?" Jason asked, trying (unsuccessfully) to keep the smile from his face. As a relatively short guy, he sometimes took a little good-natured ribbing from me about his height. Now it was payback time, as he sauntered happily through the doorway without having to duck. I, on the other hand, had gotten my clock well and truly cleaned.

Kayla had swept gracefully through the doorway with just the slightest swish of her dress. Inviting us to sit down on the bench seats that lined one of the walls, she told us to make ourselves comfortable and suggested that we deploy our digital voice recorders to see whether any of the Farnsworth's spirits would speak to us.

It was here in the attic that Kayla had her first rather frightening experience at the Farnsworth House. She was escorting a late-night tour group around the place. It was just shy of midnight when they finally came up to the attic. Her guests had taken seats on the same benches that we were now sitting on. Kayla closed the door behind them, and took up her usual position in the center of the room.

She had begun talking about some of the Civil War-era

artifacts that filled the glass display cases mounted against the opposite wall: swords in scabbards, caps, and various other memorabilia from combatants on either side.

A loud, drawn-out creaking sound stopped Kayla mid-sentence. Every head turned to face the attic door, which had spontaneously popped open, and was now slowly swinging wide on its hinges.

Kayla walked across the attic and stuck her head out onto the landing. Nobody was standing on the staircase. Nor had they heard any footsteps. Slightly puzzled, she reached out and pulled the door shut once more, thinking, *Well, **that** was strange…* She made sure that it was closed fully, hearing it click firmly into place.

Returning to the center of the room, she cleared her throat and prepared to address her audience again.

For the second time, the door opened all by itself.

"These guys are keeping themselves busy tonight," she said, passing it off as a joke.

The tourists chuckled, but here was a definite edge of nervousness to the laugh.

Deciding that enough was enough, Kayla went back to the door and closed it again. This time, she put into place the little iron horseshoe latch which prevented the door from being opened. This was a simple device that hooked over the handle. She didn't normally use it on tours, not only because the attic door had never opened by itself before — at least, not in Kayla's presence — but also because it had a habit of getting stuck in place from time to time.

The latch proved its usefulness this time, allowing Kayla to get through her entire spiel without interruption. Then, just as he had finished speaking, the attic echoed with a loud *ker-pling*.

Once again, everybody turned to look. The curved metal latch had somehow managed to flip itself up, and swung itself through 180 degrees, coming to rest in its original position.

Then the door swung open again...

Except this wasn't the gentle, almost leisurely motion that Kayla and her group had just witnessed twice before. This time, the door was flung open with such force that it slammed into the sturdy wooden chest that sat behind it, bouncing off it with a violent crash that made both Kayla and some of the guests jump.

Although she wasn't going to admit it publicly, the incident scared her. It was something that couldn't possibly be explained away with a conventional explanation...

…and it hadn't felt all that friendly, either.

Her first instinct was to hustle the group outside, go back down the staircase, and outside the building. Her guests, however, had other ideas. Now fully convinced that the attic was haunted, they all but begged Kayla to close the door and switch out the lights.

Not wanting to tempt fate, yet also wanting to keep the customers happy, Kayla reluctantly did as she was asked. Going back across the room, she closed the door once again, then reached out a hand that was shaking ever so slightly, and flipped the light switch.

The attic was plunged into darkness.

For the next few minutes, Kayla just stood there. She could hear her own heartbeat thumping away in her chest. The sound of shifting bodies and the occasional clearing of a throat came from the direction of the benches.

She tried calling out, asking the spirits of the Farnsworth House to speak to her. If the ghosts of those Confederate snipers *were* present that night, as the shenanigans with the door seemed to suggest, then those spirits were reluctant to speak.

All was still and quiet.

The sudden knocking on the attic door caught Kayla off-guard. She put a hand to her chest in an attempt to calm herself.

Oh my goodness, she thought to herself, *Mike's already here with the next tour group.*

Except, she realized even as she was unlatching the door and opening it, they hadn't heard any footsteps on the staircase…

…which was completely deserted.

Kayla would go on to have numerous other encounters with the spectral residents of the Farnsworth House over the years, but this was the one specific incident that truly convinced her that the supposed haunting was a genuine one.

Until that time, she had managed to write off each bizarre occurrence as being something perfectly natural — the building cooling down after a hot day, for example, or her imagination playing tricks on her.

But this was a bridge too far. What had just happened to Kayla up in the attic was unequivocally, undeniably paranormal in nature, and what's more, it had been witnessed by an entire group of people.

After that, she was always just a little bit wary when she went into the attic, especially when she was on her own.

Jason, Anna, and I resolved to treat the attic with every

bit of the respect that it deserved. As I crouched down to trace the length of an under-floor electrical power cable with my EMF meter (it's important to rule out false positives) I marveled at the fact that these were the original floor-boards. We were treading on the very same planks of wood that those Confederate soldiers had duck-walked on when they were going back and forth to the garret window, firing their rifles at the Union troops on Cemetery Hill. Just the mere thought of it made my mind boggle.

I reached out and rested my fingertips on the floor, then ran them slowly across the coarse grain of the wood. Men had stood, fought, bled, and, it is entirely possible, died on this floor. How much of their energy still remained here, somehow impressed on the environment by some paranormal process that we did not yet understand?

The air in the attic was hot and close, unsurprising when one remembered that not only was this summer in Gettysburg, but also that heat tends to rise.

We started running a couple of EM pumps, putting out a constant stream of electromagnetic energy into the surrounding air. I've always found this particular device (as with most gadgets used for paranormal field research) to be of questionable value. The theory goes something along the lines of: if ghosts are beings composed of pure energy, of a type that we do not yet understand, then they may be capable of using energy sources in order to sustain themselves, and perhaps manifest physically in our material world.

Ask any paranormal investigator, and they'll tell you that sudden, unexplained battery drains tend to go hand-in-hand with paranormal phenomena starting to take place. That has certainly been my experience; when a set of fresh-out-of-the-packaging Duracells go dead in no time at all, that's usually when things are going to start happening, paranormally speaking. The EM pumps were intended to offer up a free buffet of potential energy for any spirits who were willing and able to use it in order to communicate with us.

We also started an SB-7 spirit box running, setting it to sweep rapidly through various radio frequencies in the hopes that we might hear the anomalous voices which sometimes come through the device when it is used in a haunted location. Its harsh, staccato crackle provided a constant, irritating audio backdrop for our investigation of the Farnsworth House attic.

While we were setting out our monitoring equipment, Kayla decided to adopt a somewhat more old-school approach, taking out a pair of dowsing rods. After establishing that the rods crossing themselves would indicate the answer 'yes,' Kayla asked whether there were any Confederate soldiers present in the attic with us.

The rods immediately crossed. In the background, the spirit box continued to crackle.

"Please point to the spot where you are standing," she requested. Without hesitation, the dowsing rods flipped around, turning to point towards one of the corners near the garret window. I turned to look — of course, there was nothing visible, but just in case, I fired off a few quick photographs, both with and without the flash.

Nothing unusual showed up when I swiped through my camera roll a few moments later. When I'd finished, it took me a moment to realize that something had changed — without my noticing it, the attic had fallen quiet. I thought at first that somebody had switched off the spirit box, but on closer inspection, it turned out that the fresh battery that had been installed in the device had 'given up the ghost' (I know, sorry) in just a few minutes.

There it was, the classic, unexplained power drain we all knew and loved.

Kayla encouraged us to ask questions. Perhaps the most

obvious one was whether any of the spirits in the attic had taken that fateful shot toward what is now known as the Jennie Wade House. The tips of the dowsing rods crossed to indicate that yes, the shot *had* come from here.

"Where, exactly?" we wanted to know.

The rods pivoted, turning to point directly toward the garret window.

Now that *was* interesting. There are essentially two schools of thought where dowsing rods are concerned. The first possibility, put forth by some paranormal investigators, is the belief that spirit entities are somehow able to manipulate the rods by working through body of the person holding them — making this a form of physical mediumship, if you will.

The second possibility is the standard, scientifically-based explanation: the rods are being moved, not by some unseen energy field or force, but rather by tiny muscular movements on the part of the person holding them. The term for these tiny movements is 'ideo-motor motions,' and they are completely controlled by the human subconscious. The person holding the dowsing rods *wants* them to work (nobody likes looking like a fool in front of others, after all) and that strong desire manifests in the form of a series of tiny vibrations in their muscles.

As with so many aspects of paranormal research, I find myself on the fence where dowsing is concerned. I do own a set of rods myself, and have used them while investigating several different locations, but as with any other method of purported spirit communication, I take what they tell me with a grain of salt.

Kayla began addressing Walter, the spirit of the soldier who had supposedly been the one to shoot Jennie Wade.

"Walter, are you up here in this attic with us?" she asked, looking all around her. "If you are, please open up the rods."

The rods duly opened.

"Walter, were you the one who killed the spirit box?"

They instantly crossed again.

While this was going on, we deployed another SB-7 spirit box and set it running in the background. Kayla asked how many soldiers were present in the attic at this time.

FIVE, a male voice immediately responded via the speaker. The dowsing rods swung to indicate agreement.

"Do you always stay here in this attic," Kayla continued, "or do you roam the house?" The rods replied in the affirmative for the first part of the question.

Things continued in the same vein for a few more minutes. Unfortunately, Kayla had to finish up for the night. We said our goodbyes and then she left. Anna, Jason, and I remained in the attic. We switched out the lights, switched off the spirit box, and started up a basic EVP question and answer session.

Rather than sticking to the standard questions ("What's your name? How old are you?" and so forth) we chose questions that were very era-specific. What did the soldiers think of General Lee? Of General Longstreet? Of Abraham Lincoln? (Although I flatly refused to be provocative in a hallowed location such as the Farnsworth House, I suspected that this particular question might stir up a disgruntled answer, if anything would).

Nothing.

Opening up the music library on my phone, I started to play the song *Dixie* (also known as *I Wish I Was In Dixie*), a perennial favorite with the men of the South during the Civil War.

As the three of us sat there in the near-total darkness of the attic, listening to the strains of a tune that had meant so much to those Confederate soldiers who had fought at Gettysburg, it was hard not to be overwhelmed with the sheer emotion of it all. It didn't take much imagination to picture a small group of them, clustered all around us in this tightly-enclosed space, watching our every move.

What must it have felt like to have been in their well-worn boots?

They would have been weary after having spent days marching and counter-marching, before holing up in the Farnsworth House, and then spending hour after hour fighting their enemies in blue. It would have been hot, sweaty, and sometimes deadly work. Exhausted, yes, but also most likely optimistic, particularly when word of the early victories reached them from the battlefield.

But then, why were these men still here, so many years after their deaths? Were they earth-bound, or had they chosen to remain here, at what may well have been the place and time of their lives that they had found to be the most significant?

Although I'm not a religious man (though I do like to think of myself as being spiritual) I closed my eyes and offered up a silent prayer for them, asking that if they needed help moving on from this place, they be helped and guided to do so.

Although things were quiet and peaceful in the attic that

night, I felt the urge to return there again, after I had gotten a little sleep.

Chapter Seven
The P-Word

My second night in the McFarlane Room was as uneventful as the first. As I was wandering through the house the following day, I encountered a visiting team comprised of two paranormal investigators. Kayla had given me a heads-up that they were around, conducting their own research, both down in the basement and upstairs in the attic.

The two investigators had apparently had an interesting time of it the night before, at a public ghost hunting event being held at the Farnsworth. While running a ghost box session, they had repeatedly heard a child's voice come through the speaker, saying the words, YES, DADDY, whenever the male investigator (Rob) would ask questions.

This had taken place in the attic, and once all of the guests had left for the night, Rob and his fellow investigator Nicole had made the most of the opportunity to go back up there — just the two of them this time — for another ghost box session. The hope was that the presence of so many members of the public had injected some energy into the atmosphere, which hopefully the spirits would be able to use in order to manifest.

Voices began coming through the device right away, including one less-than-friendly male voice which continually said the word PRICK whenever Rob was speaking.

I was intrigued, to say the least. Always happy to meet some like-minded people, I asked whether they would object to my joining them upstairs in the attic later on that night. They graciously agreed to my request, and so at 2:30 in the morning I headed on up there.

Opening the creaky attic door (and narrowly avoiding braining myself on the doorframe) I ducked inside and flipped on the light switch. I was the first one to arrive, and although I had heard the sound of the investigators running some kind of spirit box up there earlier on, it seemed as if they had taken a break.

I sat down on one of the benches and fell quiet, just letting my senses attune to the environment that surrounded me. I looked across toward the garret window, picturing one of the many Confederate snipers who were posted in this house, kneeling there and taking potshots at Union soldiers just a little way up the street on the fringes of Cemetery Hill.

It must have been bloody cramped in here, not to mention the smell...gunpowder...stale sweat...fear...and blood.

The creak of approaching footsteps on the staircase heralded the arrival of both Kayla and my two companions for the next investigative session.

"You beat us up here," said Rob, as he opened the door and poked his head inside the attic. He was accompanied by Nicole. Together, the pair of them came in and took a seat on the bench alongside me. "So, what do you feel like doing...a standard recording session, a ghost box session, or something else?"

We debated the merits of both techniques for a few minutes. As things turned out, Rob and Nicole had taken one of the Farnsworth House ghost tours a few weeks prior to going back there, and had gotten several EVPs on the recorders that they carried around with them.

For example, when they had asked whether they ought to go directly to the basement from the attic, or whether they ought to stop off first at the Sara Black Room, an EVP had responded with the words: YES, YES, YES.

"My team has gotten some of its best results when we are just sitting around BSing," I said, "rather than asking the typical, formal EVP questions."

"Us too!" Nicole agreed. "We get the best evidence when we're not concentrating."

It was time to get started. Rob fired up the spirit box and started it scanning its way through radio frequencies. Once it was up and running, the four of us carried on talking, swapping a few funny anecdotes back and forth. At the end of one such story, we all burst out laughing.

LAUGHTER, said an asexual-sounding voice from the spirit box.

"Yes, we *are* laughing," Nicole agreed.

"It was funny," added Rob, looking around the attic.

The conversation turned a little more serious when we began discussing the subject of UFOs. I had a book soon due to be published on the subject of UFOlogy, and both Nicole and Rob had some experience in the field. I voiced the opinion that UFOlogists, cryptozoologists, and paranormal investigators had a lot more in common than most of us realized — in other words, it was possible that we were all looking at different facets of the same phenomenon.

"It's all a part of the spectrum that we call 'the unknown,'" Nicole agreed, before turning to the spirit box and asking, "What do you guys think of that?"

The same voice that had said the word LAUGHTER spoke again, but this time, its words were garbled and unintelligible.

"That's interesting," Rob mused. "It's the same voice that spoke before—"

PRICK! piped up a male voice.

That was a little embarrassing, but Rob was totally unfazed, explaining that this particular swear word was one that he had been called many times before via the same method of spirit communication — in fact, it had happened to him on no less than *ten* investigations in a row! He had also been called the same thing just the night before, right there in the attic of the Farnsworth House.

Many people (primarily those of a skeptical nature) dismiss devices such as the spirit box out of hand, insisting that because it is basically a radio frequency scanner, the so-called 'EVP' responses are nothing more than chopped-up segments of commercial radio stations, broadcasting on either the AM or FM band. That plainly could not have been true in this case, because the word 'prick' is considered to be an obscenity, and any radio station allowing such a word to be broadcast would be heavily fined — up to and including the risk of losing their license — by the FCC (Federal

Communications Commission). Whoever had just insulted Rob, certainly wasn't broadcasting on any legitimate commercial radio show.

I had just finished pointing that out when the same voice repeated, PRICK!

"Say that word for a third time," Rob asked politely. "Please and thank-you."

PRICK!

We looked at one another, dumbfounded. Third time's the charm, as the old saying went. This time, Rob had been insulted on cue, at his own request. There was no way I was buying into the idea of that being a coincidence.

During a spirit box session the night before, Rob had been called a 'butthole,' a 'disgrace,' and 'an embarrassment.' It seemed that somebody on the other side of the veil didn't like him all that much.

"What did you say in return?" I wanted to know.

"I said 'thank you,'" Rob smiled, clearly not taking it to heart.

From out of nowhere, I had a sudden moment of startling realization. Something must have shown on my face, because my companions gave me a quizzical look. "I first saw the garret of the Farnsworth House on some History

Channel documentary, maybe fifteen or twenty years ago," I explained. "Not once did it ever occur to me that one day, I would find myself sitting up here, in the best of company, being called a prick by dead people!"

It really was a surreal moment for me, and one that remind me just how lucky I am to live the life that I do, sometimes.

DONE, said a voice from the spirit box. Were the communicators trying to tell us that they were done talking to us for the night?

Apparently not, because after a couple of minutes, a male suddenly said, HE'S THERE. Just a split-second later, a second man's voice followed up with, I'M THERE.

More gobbledygook followed.

"I don't get the 'prick' thing," mused Rob.

PRICK, the same male voice repeated, followed by a second, which said, THAT'S YOU.

"Is this man a prick?" I asked, pointing directly at Rob.

YES.

"Okay…am I a prick?"

No answer.

Living in the 21st century, as we do, the work 'prick' has a very graphic, insulting connotation, in addition to being considered a very strong insult. Facing up to my own personal biases, I have to admit that I had gone into our EVP session expecting that, if we made contact with any spirit entities, they would be the spirits of long-dead Confederate soldiers, possibly those who had been killed on July 2nd and 3rd, 1863. But it was obvious to me that nobody from that particular time period would have used such a contemporary insult.

Unless...

I decided to do a little research, and was surprised to learn that the word was actually employed as a term of endearment, and that in the 19th century, 'prick' became interchangeable with 'fool' or 'idiot.' In other words, a person living during the 1800s might refer to somebody fondly as a silly prick, and mean it in the context of affection or good-natured resignation. Those same Confederate soldiers would have been very familiar with the term, and it would have been much less scathing to them than it is to us today.

"Are there any children here?" Rob had decided to change tack, and who could blame him? What sounded a lot like a young child's voice responded with: DAD! He asked who the child was, but got no answer to that.

Once again, we had to ask, what were the odds of a young child being on an AM radio station, especially at three o'clock in the morning...

We kept trying to communicate, but no more intelligible voices came through. "If you're all done, we're going to go," Nicole said.

YES, agreed a voice. After that, we got nothing further.

There had been a lot of food for thought during this EVP session. For starters, the identity of the communicators was the biggest unknown. There is a tendency among most paranormal investigators to assume that whoever one is speaking with via a spirit box, is an entity that is native to that location — in other words, it would be perfectly natural for us to jump to the conclusion that we had just talked with the spirits of the Farnsworth House...and who knows, maybe we had. But it was equally likely, in my experience, that we had been talking to an entity that one of us had brought along with us — in other words, an attachment, some kind of psychic hitch-hiker that had latched on to us at another haunted location and come along for the ride. Either Kayla, Rob, Nicole, or myself might be the unwitting host for such an entity. Without any clear evidence, it was impossible to tell.

We shook hands and called it a night. Kayla secured the attic door behind us. I didn't have too far to go, what with my new room – the Sara Black Room – being just one flight of stairs down. After washing up and climbing into the four-poster bed, I pulled the covers up to my chin and tried my hardest to ignore the spectral-looking wedding dress that seemed to float at the edge of the mattress, just beyond my feet.

Chapter Eight

Battle of the Brickyard

Flash back to the convention in Texas.

"What areas do you cover on your Gettysburg battlefield tours?" I asked Brad Klinge. We were kicking back at our respective signing tables, watching the world go by and talking a little Civil War history. During the paranormal events he ran that were open to the public, Gettysburg enthusiast Brad Klinge liked nothing more than to run a few visits to some of the hotspots and notable sites of the campaign.

Brad didn't even need a second to think about his answer. "We hit all the usual places. Devil's Den. Little Round Top. Cemetery Ridge. But then there's the places that don't get enough love."

"Like where?" I asked.

"Well, like the Brickyard, for starters." Brad could see from the look on my face that I didn't know what he was talking about. He referred to it as *the* Brickyard — in the singular sense — as though I ought to have heard of it before. "Kuhn's Brickyard. Scene of a nasty, brutal fight on the first day. A whole union brigade got ripped to shreds, right there on the north-eastern side of the town."

"That's news to me."

"It's not mentioned in a lot of the history books, but you should definitely read up on the brickyard fight," he said, reaching for a pen so he could sign another autograph. "Even today, it's a heck of a place. Next time you're there, you should look it up and see for yourself."

(Readers wishing to read a detailed account of the brickyard fight are directed to the excellent books *Gettysburg's Coster Avenue: The Brickyard Fight and the Mural* by Mark H. Dunkelman, and *Gettysburg: The First Day* by Harry W. Pfanz).

Today, the site of what was once Kuhn's Brickyard sits next to some private residences and a warehouse, located just off North Stratton Street. Things would have looked significantly different on July 1st, 1863, when this relatively small stretch of land was the scene of a bloodbath that cost the Union and Confederate forces involved a combined total of 778 casualties.

It was easy enough to find on the map, and after grabbing lunch that day, Jason and I set out to pay the place a visit.

"Brad was right," I said to Jason, stepping out of the rental car and closing the door behind me. "Just look at this place. It's *amazing*."

"Sure enough," he agreed. Together, we walked slowly across a long, sloping stretch of neatly-cropped grass. Off to our right was a huge mural, depicting the armed combat that had taken place on this very spot. It was painted on the side of what looked to be an industrial warehouse of some sort. Several stone regimental monuments stood in front of it, indicating the initial positions of the Union infantry regiments that had struggled to hold onto this terrain, before becoming hopelessly overwhelmed.

On two other sides of the enclosure, there stood a pair of houses. I could only assume that the owners of both properties knew exactly what had happened on the site of their new homes when they had bought them, and were okay with the fact that so many brave young men had died there in the summer of 1863. I don't know how comfortable I would have been living on a stretch of ground like that, to be perfectly honest, but different strokes for different folks...

"We need to come back here and run an EVP session," I said, thinking out loud. "Late at night, when there's less traffic on the roads and these neighborhoods are quieter."

And that's exactly what we did, later that night. It was a quarter 'til midnight, and Jason and I wanted to get away from the Farnsworth House for a little while. What better time to visit the site of the Battle of the Brickyard? It wasn't part of the Gettysburg battlefield *per se*, which meant that there was no moratorium on visiting the place after dark. Nevertheless, we were both very aware that this was a residential neighborhood, and didn't want to disturb any of the people who lived there, most of whom would probably be in bed by now.

We parked the car a few blocks away and walked, enjoying the somewhat cooler night air. We knew that we had come to the right place once more when Jason spotted a cannon-ball embedded in the brickwork of one of the nearby houses. It was only a few hundred feet further until we came to the site of the brickyard once more.

Keeping our voices down to a respectful and hushed whisper, we made our way to the patch of ground that marked the flank of the 154th New York, and then sat down in the grass. Each of us started a digital voice recorder running, in the hope of capturing an EVP or two. Crickets were chirping all around us, injecting their own unique brand of noise contamination, but it still seemed like a good idea to try anyway.

The air was still and calm, with little more than the occasional light breeze to ruffle our hair and clothing. Despite the fact that there were homes on either side of us, there was still an almost-indefinable sense of the sacred about this place. It, too, was hallowed ground, where men wearing both the blue and the gray had given their lives for their country. Yet there was nothing spooky or chilling about it; if anything, the calmness and tranquility were relaxing. I could very easily have lain back and gone to sleep, which is usually a pretty strong indicator that nothing paranormal was going to happen that night.

I looked off in the direction of the nearest house, which sat where the main axis of the Confederate advance had come through, and tried to put myself in the boots of those young boys in blue. What must it have felt like, I wondered, to see so many gray jackets coming right at you, each one carrying a musket or a rifle, most of which were tipped with wickedly sharp bayonets? It must have felt like standing in the path of an oncoming express train.

Then there would have been the fear — the constant fear of getting shot, or spitted on the end of a sword or a bayonet.

On the first afternoon of the battle —July 1st — the Union forces, deployed defensively to the north and west of the town, had held the enemy off for as long as they could manage. Sorely pressed by an aggressive opponent that outnumbered them significantly, the blue-coated line soon began to buckle under the strain.

When the Confederates launched a sledgehammer blow against their right flank, the Union troops began to give ground, falling back on what they hoped would be a more defensible position closer to the town. Sensing blood, the Confederates pushed forward, driving their enemy back and keeping up the pressure.

On the southern outskirts of town, near the Evergreen Cemetery and the aptly-named Cemetery Hill (for many of these young men would soon be dead themselves) sat four Union regiments: two from New York (the 134th & 154th) and two from Pennsylvania (the 27th & 73rd). The soldiers were foot-sore, having 'marched to the sound of the guns' earlier that morning. Their commanding officer, one Colonel Charles Coster, had expected to be thrown into the fight immediately, but to his surprise, his brigade had instead been ordered to wait.

Every commander likes to have a reserve force available,

acting as a kind of battlefield insurance policy against unforeseen events taking place. Based on the fact that their brothers-in-arms to the north of town were now falling back — indeed, some were fleeing, rather than retreating — the infantrymen knew that it could not be long before their services were called upon. They hurriedly wolfed down such rations as they had, lounging amongst the gravestones and waiting to be called.

They didn't have long to wait. Orders soon came down from above: the brigades that had been deployed to the north and west of Gettysburg would be heading their way, moving south toward Cemetery Hill, which was going to become a defensive bulwark against the oncoming gray tide. The problem was, those Union forces were spent. They had fought their hearts out all day long, and were now tired, hungry, and demoralized...not to mention the fact that the Confederates were snapping at their heels, and would be right behind them every step of the way.

Coster's assigned mission was a simple one. He was to take his brigade north into the town and delay the Confederate advance, covering his comrades long enough for them to get away and regroup on the southern outskirts of Gettysburg.

The New Yorkers and Pennsylvanians may have been tired, but they were still more than willing to fight. The four regiments set off at a fast clip, wending their way through the streets of the town.

Only then did the scale of the Union defeat become apparent. While Coster's units kept their formation as best they could, they were moving upstream in the face of a constant flow of retreating Federals, all of whom looked much the worse for wear. Some were wounded, and were being helped along by comrades; others had lost their weapons, or were forced to use them as crutches. Most of the faces Coster's men passed, wore the look of beaten men.

Behind them came the Confederate steamroller.

Although it lies within a built-up section of town today, the site of what would become the last stand of Coster's brigade was located on the north-eastern outskirts of Gettysburg in 1863, close to the railway station. The conjunction of two roads formed a Y, to the east of which was a brickyard owned by a man named John Kuhn.

Jason and I had looked at photographs of the area that had been taken back then, and as former soldiers ourselves, we were both struck by the fact that it did not look like a particularly strong defensive position. The terrain itself was bald and offered little in the way of cover for the three Union regiments that formed in line abreast there (the fourth regiment, the 73rd Pennsylvania, had been left back a short distance) — but in front of them were a number of fields, which would mask the movements of their enemy until the very last minute.

The ground sloped gently downward. As we sat there in the grass, gazing off in the direction from which the Confederate advance would have come and quietly asking EVP questions, my watch told me that it was now midnight. All was still calm and peaceful, but I could easily imagine the anxiety those boys must have felt as thousands of Rebel soldiers suddenly appeared in front of them, battle flags raised high. It would have been a moving gray wall, one that bristled with muskets, rifles, swords, and bayonets...one that grew closer with every passing second.

Outnumbered by at least three to one, there was no way that the Union soldiers could have held out for long. Had they known at the time that they were being placed on the chopping block, I wondered, their lives being thrown away in exchange for delaying the Confederate advance for just a short time?

The fight, when it came, was short and brutal. Coster's men gave a good account of themselves, opening fire on the Confederates as soon as they came within range, but they were caught in a pincer, with enemy soldiers returning fire on them from multiple directions at the same time. Such a heavy weight of lead slammed into the Union lines that the soldiers were scythed down in rows, as if they were nothing more than stalks of corn.

The opposing battle lines traded fire, but in the end, quantity had a quality all of its own. Having weakened their opponents with massed volley fire, the attacking Confederates charged. The hand-to-hand melee combat was, if anything, even more brutal than the musketry duel had been. Boots and bayonets took more lives, whittling the anemic Union regiments down still further.

Seeing the tactical situation deteriorate, Colonel Coster gave the order for the three regiments battling it out in Kuhn's Brickyard to retreat. Unfortunately, the runner he dispatched to convey this order was felled by a bullet after passing it on to the commanding officer of the 27th Pennsylvania, who formed the far left of the line (closest to the road). To their right, the men of the two New York regiments could only look on in horror as their left flank melted away, not knowing that a general retreat had been called.

Realizing that if they stayed in place, they would be surrounded, the New Yorkers followed suit, the officers did their best to extricate their regiments and shepherd them back to the road. It was a messy, bloody process, and by the time it was done, Coster's brigade had been utterly gutted.

Something akin to a game of hide-and-go-seek throughout the streets of Gettysburg ensued, as the broken Union regiments dispersed and tried to make good their escape. It became a case of every man for himself. Confederates hounded them at every turn, hunting their quarry each step of the way. When the weary and bloodied survivors finally reassembled back at Cemetery Hill, it soon became apparent that hundreds of Coster's men had been killed or taken prisoner.

Now Jason and I understood why the avenue we had walked down was named after him: Coster Avenue.

I asked if there were any soldiers present — from either side of the battle — that wanted to talk to us. The only sound was that of a car passing by in the near distance.

"Can any of you give us your name?" Jason asked. Crickets. Quite literally, crickets, were all that answered him.

A sudden, unexpected scream took us both by surprise. We both looked toward what had been the right end of the Union line, where the noise had seemed to originate. It had been shrill, and it was entirely possible that it had been made by a nocturnal critter of one sort or another.

Getting slowly to our feet, we walked downhill toward the right flank of the 154th regiment, hoping to track down the source of the cry. Everything was peaceful and quiet. We could only go so far without trespassing on private property, something we were naturally unwilling to do. Jason and I stood there in a pool of shadow, listening intently to the chirping crickets.

Nothing stirred.

We went back to conducting our EVP session, going on respectfully for another fifteen minutes before heading in the direction of the Confederate route of approach, and began to ask more questions.

Still nothing.

Playing back the audio recordings, we heard nothing anomalous whatsoever. After a little more than an hour, we gave up. Bidding goodbye to the former brickyard, I was in two minds about the fact that we hadn't gotten any EVPs.

On the one hand, there was the inevitable disappointment that always accompanies a fruitless session; yet on the other, there was the supposition that perhaps there had been no voice communication because there were no spirits to be found at that particular part of the battlefield — the implication being that they had all moved on, and none of them were earthbound at the place of their death.

That, at least, was a source of great solace. It was getting late, and nothing strange seemed to be happening. Time to head back to the Farnsworth House — but Jason and I had just one stop to make first.

Chapter Nine

The Children of the Battlefield

As with practically every engagement of the Civil War, whether large or small, the Gettysburg campaign has more than its share of human tragedies. The fight at Kuhn's Brickyard was no exception, and gave rise to one of the most widely-known stories of the war: that of the 'Children of the Battlefield.'

When the dust had finally settled, and the brickyard was in the hands of the Confederates, their victorious brigades resumed the offensive. When advance elements reached the intersection of York Street and Stratton Street, they found the body of a dead Union soldier. Nothing unusual about that, one might think, but clutched in his hand was an ambrotype photograph depicting three solemn-looking children. The soldier's eyes, though glazed in death, were seen to be fixed on the image. The faces of those children would have been the last thing he ever saw.

The Confederates passed on by, having better things to concern themselves with than the enemy dead. Once the battle was over, however, the victors, along with the good people of Gettysburg, had to contend with thousands of corpses from either side. While those who wore gray were given short shrift, those of the Union men were given a hasty burial whenever it was possible to do so.

Because his identity was unknown, the soldier was buried in a nameless plot. If things had gone differently, that may well have been the end of it. He would have finished up as just one more unknown soldier in a cemetery that was filled with hundreds of them.

But then, fate intervened. The photograph passed through several different sets of hands, and each time, it raised questions: who were the children, and who was the dead man that had taken their picture along with him into battle?

A written description of the ambrotype ultimately made its way into the newspapers, starting with those in Philadelphia, before spreading throughout the northern states. Finally, it reached the lap of a very anxious wife and mother.

Philinda Humiston recognized the description of the children in the picture immediately. Those were *her* three children: Franklin (8) Alice (6) and Fredrick (4). Philinda's husband, Amos, had carried such a photograph with him during his service with the 154th New York, a regiment of volunteer infantry. She knew this because she had been the one who had sent it to him.

Amos Humiston was a steady, dependable soldier. He and his regiment had proven themselves in battle, perhaps most notably at the bloodbath known as Chancellorsville, where the 154th took heavy casualties while trying to fend off a flank attack. Amos himself only narrowly avoided being killed. He was not so fortunate at Kuhn's Brickyard.

Once Sergeant Humiston was identified as the father of the three children in the photograph, his grave was properly marked with a tombstone bearing his name. Philinda was finally able to get closure, something denied to thousands of other war widows on either side of the conflict, whose loved ones simply never returned from battle, and presumably ended up in an unmarked grave far from home.

Perhaps more importantly, the story of the Humiston family drew greater public awareness of a crucial issue: the plight of the children of the battlefield, those poor kids that were orphaned by the war and had nowhere to go. Charitable funds were raised, and Gettysburg received its own orphanage in which to accommodate them, which could be found just a stone's throw away from the Farnsworth House. The orphanage developed a reputation for brutally mistreating the children who lived there, under the auspices of a vile woman named Rosa Carmichael. She liked nothing better than to see the children viciously beaten, either by herself, or by an older child, and thought nothing of chaining them to the cellar walls in absolute darkness for hours on end.

Carmichael was ultimately fined (she got off lightly — cruelty such as she had shown to those orphans should have landed her in jail) and the orphanage subsequently closed. The orphans were placed with families who almost certainly treated them better than their malign overseer ever had.

Not far from the Gettysburg fire house is a simple memorial stone. Jason and I had no trouble finding it. Three small American flags were planted in the dirt in front of the stone, which was placed as close as possible to the spot where Amos Humiston's body had been found.

We each took a knee, more out of respect for Amos's memory than for ease of reading the words on the plaque, which contained engraved images of Amos Humiston and the faces of his three children. I am not a religious man (though I do consider myself to be spiritual) but I closed my eyes for a moment, and offered up a prayer for Amos's soul, in the hopes that he and his family had been reunited in the afterlife.

"Damn," Jason said quietly, lost in his own thoughts.

Finally, after paying our respects, we made our way back to the Farnsworth House. That wasn't the end of it, however. For days afterward, I couldn't get the story of Amos Humiston and the 154th New York out of my head.

I dealt with it by writing a short story about him, and the battle for Kuhn's Brickyard. It was titled *Blood and Bricks*, and if you would care to read it, it has been included as an extra feature at the end of this book.

Chapter Ten

The Sara Black Room

When I contacted the Farnsworth House in order to book my stay there and to request permission to conduct a paranormal investigation, I specifically requested the most haunted room. The member of staff that I spoke with had no hesitation in recommending the Sara Black Room, saying that it was almost certainly the most paranormally active part of the Farnsworth House, with the possible exception of the cellar, which is not a guest room.

"I'll take it," I said instantly. A host of ghost stories and lore surround this particular room, and I reasoned that even if only half of them had a basis in truth, then I would be moving into one of the most haunted rooms in Gettysburg, if not the whole country.

Ownership of the Farnsworth House left the Sweney family in 1909, and passed to George Black and his wife Verna. A local man born and bred, George had served with an infantry regiment during the Civil War, and worked for the Postal Service in Gettysburg. The steady stream of visitors coming to tour the Gettysburg battlefield caught Verna Black's eye. Sensing an opportunity, she convinced her husband to convert the former Sweney House into a place of lodging in 1918 or thereabouts, naming it the Sleepy Hollow Lodge.

This particular room is named after the daughter of the Blacks, one Sara Black Gideon, who became the owner of the house in 1959 following the deaths of both of her parents. During her time there, it would have been the master bedroom of the house.

Of the many paranormal encounters that guests and visiting investigators claim to have experienced in the room, the vast majority seem to center around the spirit of Jeremy. It is said that the five year-old Jeremy was playing games in the street outside the Farnsworth House one day, dashing out to tag horses, carts, and carriages as they went past. This simple case of 'boys will be boys' was a dangerous pastime (which was doubtless what made it seem so appealing) and poor Jeremy paid the ultimate price when one of the speeding horses accidentally hit him, inflicting grievous injuries from which he would never recover.

As the story has it, Jeremy's father came immediately to his son's aid, but the wounds were so severe that the poor boy was beyond saving. Carrying his son's lifeless body into the house, Jeremy's father took it into what was then the nursery, but is now the bathroom of the Sara Black Room, where he is said to have spent the next few hours weeping inconsolably over the loss of his boy.

Just how much of this story is grounded in fact is unclear. It has been part of the Farnsworth House ghost lore for many years, however, and the fact remains that countless visitors have reported encountering the ghost of a young child throughout the house, along with the apparition of a sorrowful-looking adult male who is presumed to be Jeremy's grieving father. Dressed in late nineteenth-century attire, this tragic figure is most often seen in the hallway outside the Sara Black Room, or sitting beside the bed in the McFarlane Room. While he never speaks to those who see him, the eyewitnesses usually state that he seems to be deeply upset about something.

Jeremy, on the other hand, is a friendly and sometimes even slightly mischievous spirit. When he isn't running around the rooms and hallways of the Farnsworth House, Jeremy likes nothing better than to play pranks upon the living. His footsteps are often heard in the hallways, and more than one guest has woken to the sound of a young boy laughing and giggling from somewhere in the shadows of the Sara Black Room.

One thing that struck me as being particularly heartwarming was the Farnsworth House tradition of visitors leaving toys and candy as an offering for Jeremy. As an aside, I had recently encountered the same thing five thousand miles away at the infamous Jamaica Inn, an old smuggler's haven located on Bodmin Moor in Cornwall, England. Made famous by the novelist Daphne Du Maurier in her novel of the same name (and later by movie maestro Alfred Hitchcock) Jamaica Inn is replete with stories of ghosts and spirits. One of the rooms (Room Five) situated in the oldest part of the inn, is said to be haunted by the spirit of a young girl named Hannah. Naturally, I requested that specific room for the duration of our stay.

After checking in to Room Five, we set about unpacking our things. On opening one of the wardrobe drawers, my wife was surprised to find it crammed full of toys and souvenirs, along with affectionate hand-written notes to the little girl's ghost. Believed to be around eleven years old, Hannah was apparently a very active entity, and the list of encounters with her would fill up an entire book. While I was away for the night investigating the haunted Bodmin Jail nearby, my wife had her own encounter with Hannah; laying in the four poster bed, she suddenly felt a tiny hand touch her several times beneath the bed clothes, before prodding her a couple of times. She made certain to speak very nicely to Hannah.

There are many accounts of Jeremy playing with the toys that have been left for him in the Sara Black Room, and I made a mental note to use some of them as control objects during the course of my investigation. I had also brought along a 'Boo Buddy,' which is a series of temperature, vibration, and EMF sensors all wrapped up in the body of a teddy bear. The idea of the Boo Buddy (which I had named 'Stephen,' after my fellow investigator and favorite ghost-hunting priest) was to entice out the spirits of children and encourage them to manifest physically. I hoped that it would help me make contact with young Jeremy, if he was around during the course of my investigation.

At first glance, it might seem that Jeremy's grief-stricken father could still be earth-bound at the Farnsworth House because of the great loss and suffering that he was forced to endure. I wasn't so sure about that; the fact that there seemed to be no accounts of the well-dressed gentleman speaking to those who saw him, or making any sort of eye contact, made me think that the forlorn apparition was most likely a residual ghost, a sort of paranormal recording that contains no more awareness or intelligence than the images that you see on your TV screen.

Jeremy, on the other hand, is fully interactive, and I would therefore classify his case as being that of an intelligent haunting. An entity which likes to play with toys, grab visitors by the ankles, and mess with their clothing has got to be something more than a simple recording, after all. I couldn't wait to see if the ghostly boy would be willing to make contact with me when I spent a couple of nights alone in the Sara Black Room.

I turned in the key to the McFarlane Room at noon on Saturday, and moved all of my stuff into the Sara Black Room just a few doors down. In terms of space, it was definitely an upgrade. The bathroom was much bigger than that in the McFarlane Room.

Just a few minutes earlier, as I was lugging my suitcases across the hall, I encountered one of the cleaning staff, and couldn't pass up the chance to ask her about her own experiences working at the Farnsworth House. During her six months of employment, she said that the spirit she encountered most often was Jeremy. She had noticed that he liked to take toys and place them in the middle of the floor when she was making up a room prior to the next guest's arrival. Although we'd had no luck so far in trying to entice Jeremy out using the Boo Buddy, I was hopeful that he might put in an appearance in this new room. We'd find out for sure later that night.

The first thing that draws the eye when you walk into the Sara Black Room is the white wedding dress that is mounted on a stand by the window. An often-told story associated with the dress is that it once belonged to a bride-to-be, who was jilted at the altar on her wedding day — this tale is an urban legend, without a grain of truth to it. Vivian, the head of housekeeping at the Farnsworth House, recalls the dress being brought in from the personal effects of a family member of the owners. Be that as it may, Guests have reported the dress taking on a life of its own, flipping the empty sleeves as if the invisible wearer was in a state of great agitation. One had to wonder whether this was one of the resident entities playing games with the guests.

As this was once Sara Black Gideon's bedroom, there are photographs and mementoes of her everywhere one looks. Her framed graduation diploma from Gettysburg High School hangs on one wall, dating back to June 7th, 1923. A monochrome photograph of the good lady herself takes pride of place directly above the pillows on the wall above the four-poster bed.

A little more disturbing is a framed memorial plaque containing photographs of a little boy and an older man, each of them wearing Victorian-era apparel. *"In loving memory, Father, Jeremy,"* the plaque states, *"Named for a former owner and noted for its intense spirit activity, the Sara Black Room is occasionally visited by a small boy whom we have come to affectionately call Jeremy — mortally wounded in a carriage accident outside the house — his grief-stricken father is still seen at the bedside, desperately seeking the help needed to save his beloved child."*

That plaque was going to be the last thing I saw at night before turning out the light.

Former tenants of the Sara Black room had left me plenty of late-night reading material, in the form of the guest book, which I found sitting on the night stand next to the bed.

After brushing my teeth and climbing into the grand old four-poster bed, which groaned beneath my not-inconsiderable weight, I sank back into what felt like a small mountain of pillows, picked up the guest book, and began to leaf through it.

I found it difficult to concentrate at first. For one thing, I was having a hard time shaking the feeling that I was being watched. While it would be easy to jump to the conclusion that one of the spirits of the Farnsworth House had dropped in to keep an eye on me, that would have been too great an assumption on my part.

For starters, there were mind games aplenty going on. I was spending the night alone in what many people claimed to be the most haunted room, at the most haunted inn, in one of the most haunted towns in the world – there was even a framed certificate on the wall to remind me of its fearsome reputation! The entire room looked as if it had been frozen in time, and I suspected that it wouldn't have looked all that different back in 1863, barring a few of the electrical devices.

My eye was constantly drawn to the wedding dress that stood at the foot of the bed. It looked for all the world like the apparition of a woman, floating in thin air just a few feet away for me. Was it my imagination, or was the dress actually moving? (The answer turned out to be yes, it *was* my imagination).

Then my gaze wandered over toward the bathroom, where young Jeremy was said to have breathed his last. Was the spirit of the young fellow still around after all these years, as so many visitors claimed? The thought that a long-dead child might pay me a nocturnal visit was more than enough to give me a case of the chills.

Just between the two of us, dear reader, I *hate* sleeping in haunted rooms. That might sound strange, given the fact that I have been doing exactly that for close to twenty-five years; the truth is that, while I'm never happier than when I'm hanging around in some old and haunted building, I really don't like going to sleep in one. It feels too much like letting my guard down, which in turn makes me feel much too vulnerable, as if I'm opening myself up to who knows what while I'm out like a light.

Oh, suck it up! I told myself, with a reminder that nobody had held me at gunpoint and forced me to do this. It was a privilege to spend a few nights in a place as historic, as full of character, as the Farnsworth House…and if things went bump in the night while I was sleeping, well, wasn't that what I had pretty much signed up for?

Doing my best to quash this case of the creeps before it

really got entrenched, I returned my attention to the guest book, which made for fascinating reading. Before long, I was engrossed. It seemed as if at least half of the guests had experienced something odd, and potentially paranormal, during their stay in this particular room.

A couple named Tom and Dawn had stayed in the Sara Black room for two nights. They had been awoken several times in the wee small hours of the morning (always been 2am and 4am) by the sound of heavy footsteps walking around on the floorboards outside their door. While it would be easy to write this off as being another guest prowling around in the middle of the night, that wouldn't explain why the footsteps were also heard coming from *inside* the room.

The couple also claimed to have communicated with the spirit of Sara Black herself, Jeremy, and Walter, who had said that he preferred to spend most of his time in the basement rather than the attic, and — in what made for a rather intriguing claim — that somebody he referred to as 'father' had performed an exorcism down there.

No sooner had they vacated the Sara Black room than another couple took their place. They reported hearing heavy dragging sounds coming from the empty attic above their heads, and one of them felt unseen hands being run through her hair in the middle of the night.

The next occupants were yet another a couple. The lady awoke at 5am and went into the restroom. While she was in there, she heard the distinct sound of footsteps walking around the four-poster bed in which her husband still slept, accompanied by two small but very clear knocks from the underside of the bed frame.

Needless to say, she declined to go back to bed after that.

Strange physical phenomena were also experienced by the next occupants of the room. They witnessed the locked door handle being jiggled, as though somebody was trying to get into the room from the outside. When they opened it up to check, there was nobody to be found either in the hallway or on the staircase outside.

The same thing happened several times throughout the night, and was often accompanied by a definite drop in the temperature within the room. The phenomenon of the sudden onset of coldness when paranormal activity starts taking place, is well-documented within the literature of paranormal research.

Another guest was woken up to the sound of what he described as 'an old-style record player,' while his wife awoke several times to the overpowering scent of perfume in the room. I can personally vouch for the fact that there are no automated air fresheners in the Sara Black room, so the origin of the smell remains a mystery.

At seven o'clock the following morning, the couple were in bed, discussing the remarkable events of the night before. Suddenly, they both heard the sound of heavy footsteps circling the bed, just as the female visitor had done a few days before. One can only imagine the stunned reaction of the two guests as the bed then began to shake, as if an invisible person was rocking it back and forth.

Displaying an admirably healthy sense of skepticism, they got out of bed and stomped around the room, trying to recreate the experience. Try as they might, they could not get the bed to shake as it had done just moments before.

The mystery was solved later that morning, when the occupants of the room next door woke up and began walking around. It turned out that whenever they would step close to the wall which separated the two rooms, the floorboards in the Sara Black room would creak in a manner redolent of what they had taken to be phantom footsteps; the bed would also vibrate. My hat goes off to this unnamed couple for their willingness to keep an open mind, and to explore non-paranormal possibilities.

One other thing that they were able to debunk was the mysterious music, which the couple traced to the chimes of the grandfather clock which stood downstairs.

The odor of perfume, however, was never satisfactorily explained.

Another guest reported the rather disconcerting experience of having their feet touched while they were lying in bed. The following morning, while sitting in a chair by the window, the guest heard the distinct clip-clop of horses' hooves outside in the street. Obviously one of the many re-enactments which take place around the Gettysburg park throughout the year was about to start.

Standing up to look outside, they were taken aback to see that there wasn't a horse in sight.

The next guests to take up residence in the Sara Black room experienced just one unusual occurrence during their three nights there — on two separate occasions, something struck the bed frame so forcefully that it made the entire bed vibrate. The couple who followed them also experienced something strange while sleeping in the four-poster bed…an invisible 'something,' as they describe it, inserted itself between them, and began to slowly push them apart to opposite sides of the mattress.

While the next couple were drifting off to sleep, at around midnight, one of them felt something grab their arm and jostle them awake once more. They were even more concerned the following morning, when they awoke to find the bottle of Advil they had brought with them lying in the floor in the middle of the room, with several of the pills scattered around it. Could this have been Jeremy, up to his usual childish antics? If so, then so much for the supposedly 'child-proof' cap on the pill bottle.

It's striking just how much of the paranormal activity taking place in the Sara Black room seems to center upon the bed. *I went to bed and turned the lights out*, one of the guests wrote. *I just got relaxed and rolled onto my stomach, when I felt something pull on the sheets as if tucking me in bed.*

Although the tragic story behind the dress doesn't have any basis in fact, it is certainly true that a number of strange occurrences have been reported involving it. One example is the guest who spent the night in the room with their daughter as a celebratory birthday treat. When the pair of them left the Sara Black room to go and enjoy dinner, followed by a ghost tour of the Farnsworth House, the top hat that lives permanently in the room was sitting on top of one of the bed posts.

When they returned from the tour, it was a little after midnight. They were startled to find that the hat was now sitting on top of the dress, looking for all the world as though it had been placed atop an invisible head!

The same guests were woken up in the middle of the night by the sound of footsteps pacing back and forth outside the room.

The mysteriously mobile top hat greeted the next set of guests in exactly the same way. What's particularly interesting is that the guest insisted that the hat had been nowhere to be found in the room when she and her boyfriend had gone to sleep. When they awakened the next morning, there it was, once again crowning the wedding dress.

As if this wasn't enough, the couple had not slept soundly during the night. The boyfriend felt something pulling the hairs on his back, which he blamed on his somewhat indignant girlfriend (she was reading at the time). When the lights went out, it was her turn for some unwanted attention. She could feel something slowly but deliberately tickling the arch of her foot. They were woken in the night several times by the sound of giggling (Jeremy again?), heard children's toys moving by themselves on the floor across the room, and the sound of footsteps walking around the bed. There is no mention of the guests in the neighboring room being up and about at the time the footsteps were heard, so this is a difficult one to validate or debunk.

Will and Steve moved in for one night, and, by their own admission, were 'laying in bed drinking cabernet sauvignon,' when there were two loud thumps on the door. This experience was repeated with the following guests, a married couple, who also heard somebody knocking on the door, as though trying to get in. When the wife was soaking in the bath, the hot water tap turned on and began to flow of its own accord.

A fascinating aspect of some hauntings is that they appear to be cyclical in nature. This is particularly true when they are centered around either a specific event, or series of events, which took place on a certain date or dates.

What often tends to happen is that the paranormal activity increases in both frequency and intensity as the date of significance approaches, before peaking on, or very close to, the time of the incident, and then waning once the event has passed. The whole cycle then repeats itself all over again the following year.

After having spoken to the staff at the Farnsworth House and reviewing some of the experiences reported by guests, this principle does indeed seem to hold true. As the July anniversary of the Battle of Gettysburg approaches, the paranormal activity intensifies at the Farnsworth (and throughout the town in general). A skeptic would rightfully point out that the summer months bring an influx of visitors, many of whom seem determined to catch sight of a ghost. They also bring an increase in the number of re-enactments taking place, and therefore the number of flesh and blood men and women wearing period dress that are wandering the streets of Gettysburg — people who are sometimes mistaken for apparitions.

After having had such a wild night in the McFarlane Room, Lisa returned for a second stay at the Farnsworth House, albeit with a different companion. This time, they spent the night in the Sara Black Room.

Lisa and her friend Chenita were looking forward to their stay, and after what had happened the last time, were not expecting to spend the night without being disturbed in one form or another. They were not to be disappointed.

The day started out quietly enough. Gettysburg in August is a busy place, bustling with sightseers and visitors from all around the world. There is a lot of energy in the air, and darkness doesn't fall until fairly late in the evening. The Farnsworth House is usually full to capacity, or close to it, which may well explain why the two ladies kept hearing footsteps walking back and forth outside their room once they had retired for the night. Whenever one of them poked their head around the door to look outside into the hallway, however, nobody seemed to be there. Whoever was walking around out there had to have been very quick on their feet.

The footsteps went on all through the night, long after most reasonable people would have gone to bed. It was distracting and a little creepy, but they both wrote it off as being one of the quirks associated with staying in a historic and haunted old building…

…until the dragging began.

The sudden noise was unexpected, coming as it did from the ceiling up above their heads. Directly above them was the attic.

"It sounded as if something heavy was being dragged

across the floor of the attic," Lisa and Chenita recalled afterward, "making the boards creak as it moved from one side of the ceiling to the other. This was very late at night, when none of the guests or staff would have had a reason to be walking around up there."

This particular dragging sound is one of the more commonly-reported paranormal phenomena at the Farnsworth House. It is believed that they are the residual sounds of those Confederate sharpshooters, who dragged furniture around in order to free up a little space.

Chenita and Lisa laughed a little nervously, unable to take their eyes off the ceiling. Was somebody messing with them, perhaps playing a prank? If so, it was an isolated event, because the dragging sounds stopped as suddenly as they had begun. The footsteps outside, however, continued unabated.

Then the phenomena began to close in, happening inside the room itself. The floorboards next to the bed, which until now had been quiet all night, started to creak. It was if an unseen person was standing there, shifting their weight from one foot to the other and back again.

Looking at it from a skeptical perspective, I would have to point out that the structure of most buildings —

particularly older ones — tend to expand during the daytime, especially on hot days, before contracting again at night when things cool down. This contraction invariably brings along with it a great deal of creaking and groaning, which can sometimes sound as if the floorboards are being trodden on. But what Chenita and Lisa described sounded different to the typical noises a building like the Farnsworth would be expected to make, and I made a mental note to look out for the phenomenon myself during my stay in the Sara Black Room, and try to determine whether it was structural in nature…or something else.

Turning out the lights, the two ladies did their best to try and get some sleep. Alas, it was not to be. Their heads had barely hit the pillow before tapping sounds began to originate from the headboard just behind Chenita's head. Although she did her best to ignore them, they didn't go away, and soon became an annoyance.

"Please stop," Chenita said, somewhat irritably. "We really need to get some sleep."

Instantly, the creaking and tapping sounds ceased.

It had been a long day, and Lisa drifted off to sleep almost immediately. Chenita, on the other hand, wasn't feeling her best. She had been suffering from a stuffy nose and a sore throat, and that made it difficult for her to nod off, especially when she was laying down flat. Nevertheless, she gave it her best shot, drifting in and out of sleep for who knows how long.

Suddenly, she felt something push down on the bottom of the bed, next to her feet. Sitting up, Chenita reached out and flipped on the light switch. She could hardly believe what she saw. Two indentations pushed down into the mattress, as though unseen hands were pressing on it from above.

"Lisa," she called out, rousing her roommate from a sound sleep. "Wake up. You have *got* to see this…"

Bleary-eyed, Lisa sat up too, and both women watched incredulously as the indentations pushed the mattress up and down a couple more times before stopping.

Chenita was excited to experience something so unusual, but the mattress soon stopped moving, and after a while both women were able to go back to sleep once more. The Sara Black Room was calm and still until three o'clock in the morning, when Chenita was woken up by the rather strange sensation of the bedclothes moving all by themselves. As she lay there, listening to the sound of Lisa softly breathing in her sleep, Chenita felt the sheets slowly but definitely tucking themselves beneath her body. It began on the left side of her chest, and worked its way down to her thigh, almost as if somebody were tucking her into bed as one might do with a child at bedtime.

As if that wasn't enough, the bathroom faucet turned itself on in the night, dumping a spray of water into the sink for a few seconds before spontaneously shutting off again, and the flashlight that they had left sitting on top of the dresser somehow managed to light up all by itself.

After Chenita managed to get back to sleep, it was Lisa's turn to get some attention from the resident ghost. Several times during the night, she was half-awoken by something that wanted to play with her hair. Drowsily, she swatted at whatever it was, rolled over, and went back to sleep. When she woke up the next morning, Lisa said that Chenita's constant whispering had made it difficult for her to sleep in the wee small hours of the morning— to which Chenita replied that she hadn't been whispering at all.

Lisa blanched on hearing the news, and asked whether Chenita had been the one to cover her up with the blankets during the night, as that is what she had assumed. Chenita had to admit that she hadn't been responsible for that either. Both girls had been covered up in the night. It appeared that their ghostly companion had taken something of a shine to them. Despite all that they had experienced, neither Lisa nor Chenita felt that there was anything frightening or negative about the Sara Black Room. Both of them very much enjoyed their overnight stay, and would be more than willing to go back — so long as they didn't have to stay in the McFarlane Room.

Jason, Anna, and I met up in the Sara Black Room for a spirit box session. We ran a standard SB-11 device, sweeping quickly through the AM radio frequencies at a very fast clip. Aside from two occasions when we called out to Jeremy, and heard what sounded suspiciously like a child's voice replying, nothing intelligible came through the device. We tried a range of questions and different approaches, with all three of us taking turns to attempt communication, all to no avail.

Then we followed up with a couple of rapid-fire, two-minute burst EVP sessions, asking a series of short questions.

Still nothing.

It appeared that the spirits of the Farnsworth House just weren't in a particularly talkative mood that night…but we were about to be proven wrong about that, when we spent some time investigating the cellar.

Chapter Eleven

Into the Cellar

One of the areas that had always fascinated me most about the Farnsworth House was its cellar.

Mr. Sweney, who owned the house at the time of the battle, is believed to have taken shelter down in the cellar, along with several other civilians.

Stop for just a moment, and think about what the conditions must have been like down there, in such a claustrophobic, enclosed space. The screams of the wounded and dying up would have been a constant soundtrack, competing with the booming of cannons and the sound of bullets and musket balls striking the walls outside.

Except for the occasional lull in the battle, there would have been no peace. No respite. The sheer psychological terror of it all is difficult for us to comprehend.

Displaying a fine flair for showmanship, the present-day staff of the Farnsworth House have dressed the cellar in the style of an undertaker's parlor, beautifully evoking the eerie, funereal atmosphere of the Civil War era.

As visitors descend the steps from street level, the first thing that usually grabs their attention tends to be the coffin at the front of the room. Look inside, and you will see the body of a man staring back at you, wide-eyed, as though he is surprised to be dead. The mannequin is startlingly life-like, especially when the cellar lights are dimmed.

A large mirror stands propped against one wall. Although it looks innocent enough, Lorraine Warren once claimed that a negative spirit entity is associated with the mirror, and that it would be wise to give it a wide berth. Be that as it may, I decided to take the risk, and snapped a photo of myself in the mirror. I was disappointed to find that nothing unusual turned up in the resulting photo.

Some visitors have reported seeing a ghostly extra standing next to them in the pictures they have taken. (Of course, it always pays to be wary of apparently ghostly images that appear in mirrors, windows, and other reflective surfaces — most often, they turn out to be nothing more than pareidolia – the brain playing tricks on itself).

Kayla had come down to the basement on numerous occasions to find the mirror covered up with a cloth (when it had been left uncovered the night before) and at other times, completely flipped around so that the glass was facing the wall. At times, it seemed to have almost taken on a life of its own.

A number of visitors to the Farnsworth House have reported seeing somebody other than themselves staring back at them when they stood in front of the mirror. Others have claimed to see a lady dressed entirely in black reflected there.

One night, Kayla's aunt happened to be visiting. She was sitting in the front row of seats, looking directly toward the mirror. Not exactly a woman given to flights of fancy, she insisted that she had seen the handprint of a small child slowly pressing itself against the glass, leaving behind an imprint of the palm and fingers that dissipated as quickly as it had appeared.

"This thing is very strange and creepy," Kayla told us, "but I've never had anything happen to me when I've looked in it. I guess that's just my good luck, because plenty of other people tell a very different story…"

Unbeknownst to us, just a few weeks after our investigation, Amy Bruni and Adam Berry from the TV show *Kindred Spirits* would base an entire episode of their show around this particular mirror.

As the episode opens, Amy and Adam are walking

through the streets of Gettysburg and discussing a few preliminary aspects of the case. Amy refers to what is happening at the Farnsworth House as "a dark haunting," implying that it is malevolent in nature. Based upon my time investigating there, I am not convinced that this is necessarily the case…but with that being said, it is a possibility that I would also not discount out of hand.

It's great to see our friend Kayla shining in this episode. She and her fellow storyteller, Steven, waste no time in directing Amy and Adam down to the cellar. It is revealed that paranormal activity at the Farnsworth House has ramped up to such an extent that two customers fled from a tour just a few days prior to this episode being shot, presumably because of what was going on down there.

(It's also interesting to note that Steven puts the number of ghosts that are believed to haunt the Farnsworth House at fourteen).

Who do they believe is responsible for haunting the basement? In Steven's opinion, it's a "curmudgeonly, older Confederate soldier," which would certainly fit with the role played by that part of the house during the battle. Kayla concurs, adding that this fellow doesn't seem to like women a great deal. This is borne out by the story of a female storyteller at the Farnsworth, who felt an invisible hand pinching her tightly on her upper arm. Despite her moving position from one part of the basement to another, the painful sensation did not cease — it kept on going, leaving a series of red marks on her skin.

Little did I know that I would soon have my own physical experience in that very same place, when my team and I spent a night in the basement of the Farnsworth House.

The negative experiences are happening more often, and so Amy and Adam set out to find out why. In the opinion of Kayla and Steven, the mirror seemed like a prime candidate.

A few weeks before, Kayla had been giving a tour of the property as usual. One of the female guests had stood in front of the mirror and taken a picture of herself. One can only imagine her reaction when she checked the photograph, only to find that a black smile had been superimposed over her own mouth.

The story of the haunted mirror is not without precedent. I was fortunate enough to work at one of the world's most haunted hotels, the historic Stanley Hotel in Estes Park, Colorado, for several years. Much like Kayla, I gave tours there, telling stories of the spirits of the Stanley to those who were fascinated by its spooky reputation.

In the basement of the Concert Hall (arguably the most paranormally active part of the entire hotel complex) was a similar mirror. It was one of the few artifacts that was not original to the Stanley, having instead been purchased and brought there, its history entirely unknown. More ghostly occurrences seemed to take place in and around that mirror than anywhere else in the building. Guests would often be shocked to find that when they took a selfie in the mirror, a phantom 'extra' would turn up in the shot. On one particularly memorable occasion, which I witnessed personally, what appears to be the shadow figure of a woman in period dress showed up in a picture, apparently floating above the ground just a few steps behind the photographer.

Mirrors have long been associated with the spirit world. Scrying, a technique which involves an observer staring into one for a prolonged amount of time, is believed by some to be a viable method of communicating with disembodied spirits. It has been used for hundreds, if not thousands, of years.

The next stop for Amy and Adam is the attic. Once again, there are accounts of female visitors being physically harassed, suffering pokes, prods, pinches, and their hair being pulled — signs of a playful entity, or something altogether more sinister? Kayla reveals that she once felt an invisible *something* breathing in her ear, seconds before a voice told her to GET OUT.

It is becoming difficult to escape the conclusion that whoever or whatever is responsible for this paranormal activity must really dislike females…after all, it seems to primarily target them for its attentions.

We are told that a number of her staff members seem to have a strong distaste for the mirror. The activity down in the basement became so bad that one of the storytellers was forced to quit her job; she had gotten on the bad side of whatever haunted that particular part of the house, and it simply would not leave the poor woman alone.

Armed with a little foreknowledge, Amy and Adam elect to spend their first night investigating the basement. They start out by conducting a spirit box session with a twist. The spirit box is a frequency-hopping radio scanner, which some people believe can allow the voices of discarnate entities to speak to the living.

I would use similar devices during my own investigation at the Farnsworth House, but the technique used by the *Kindred Spirits* team is a little different. It is known as 'the Estes Method,' named after the town of Estes Park,

Colorado, where members of the Stanley Paranormal Investigation Team used it regularly while investigating the Stanley Hotel.

As I write these words (March of 2019) the Estes Method is very much in vogue among members of the paranormal research community. One participant — in this case, Amy Bruni — is blindfolded, and given a set of headphones that shut out as much ambient noise as possible. These headphones are connected directly into the spirit box itself, usually an SB-7 or SB-11 model, both of which are extremely popular. The second participant acts as the questioner, calling out to whichever entities might be listening in. The first person deliberately has most of their external sensory stimuli cut off; their only job is to listen to the spirit box input, and to verbalize whatever meaningful words or phrases they might hear.

When things go well, as they sometimes do, it is entirely possible for the participant doing the listening to deliver answers to questions that they could not possibly have heard with their own ears (and the blindfold was placed in order to prevent them from lip-reading)

Amy's responses are, frankly, rather vague and generic during this session. Words and phrases such as "You never know," "Maybe," and "listen," really don't tell us a great deal. One incident is a little more interesting. Adam asks if the spirits can turn a flashlight on, which does indeed happen, followed by Amy saying the word "yes."

The so-called "flashlight technique" (also known as the flashlight trick) doesn't have a lot of value when you use a Maglite-style flashlight, because it has a very simple scientific explanation: small fluctuations in temperature cause parts of the light to expand and contract, completing the electrical circuit and making the light switch itself on and off. It's easy, skeptics say, to misconstrue this for spirit communication. On the other hand, those who advocate for the technique like to point out that sometimes the timing of such on/off changes seems a little *too* perfect, and therefore an entity might be manipulating the flashlight after all. Although it's impossible to say for sure which is which in a specific case, there's enough doubt around this technique that my team and I have stopped using it.

Amy and Adam then make a side-trip to the attic, only to find absolutely nothing happening up there. I have a lot of sympathy for them in that regard. In what seems like a wise move, they decided to focus on the cellar in general, and the mirror in particular. Not a lot is known about its history, mainly because it was picked up at an estate sale and brought back to the house. An expert dates the mirror frame as being post-Civil War, probably sometime around the early 1900s, and the glass to the 1950s or 1960s. The mirror was obviously broken at some point, and had to have the pane of glass replaced.

In an unconventional (and, I think, inspired) turn of events, they decide to head to the former orphanage just a stone's throw away from the Farnsworth House, with a view to asking the other spirits of Gettysburg for some help with this particular case.

They pick up a figure on the Structured Light Sensor (SLS) camera. Depending on your beliefs, this could either be an unseen entity or a false-positive; SLS cameras often mistake vertical lines, such as doorframes, standing lamps, and other such things, as being human shapes. Amy and Adam take the view that this was a spirit entity, trying to hold Amy's hand. No light is shed on the Farnsworth Haunting, however, so they head to the Jennie Wade House next.

They get a couple of EVPs which imply that there may be a newer entity at the Farnsworth House – one which is associated with the mirror.

Some historical research traces the mirror back to a local farm. One of the members of the family which owned the farm was involved with trafficking women, and also was responsible for murdering a Gettysburg tour guide in 1918. The murderer went to the gallows three years later. Could there be a connection with the mirror?

Enter guest investigators Greg and Dana Newkirk, who agree to help investigate the mirror. The Newkirks help create a *psychomanteum,* a means by which the living may be able to communicate with the dead. Because the negative entity is said to prey upon women, Amy and Dana put themselves into a trance state, with candlelight and white noise as background.

Observing the experiment, Greg and Adam witness what seems to be an unexplained flash of light emanating from the mirror – which mimicked our own experience in the cellar, a few weeks earlier.

Amy was seen to touch her neck, and says that she felt something touching her throat…and choking her. She also claims to have seen a male face with a white collar. Dana states that she saw the same thing. Whether this was genuinely paranormal, or simply Dana and Amy's own minds paying tricks upon them, is impossible to say, but when a photograph of the murderer is shown to them, Dana and Amy positively identify him as the man whose face she saw.

They conclude that the spirit of the killer, a man named Clarence Collins, is attached to the mirror, and advise the owners of the Farnsworth House to get rid of it. This advice was taken, and today, the mirror can no longer be found in the cellar of the house.

The episode of *Kindred Spirits* wasn't Amy and Adam's first visit to the basement of the Farnsworth House. They had both spent some time down there a few years before, filming an episode of *Ghost Hunters*.

Both investigators claimed to see some kind of dark mass moving around down there, as did their colleagues Jason Hawes and Steve Gonsalves, who went down to the cellar afterward. By all accounts, this was going to be a hotspot, and as Kayla told us about the ghostly experiences that she and her fellow storytellers had in that part of the building, Jason, Anna, and I sat quietly, our eyes constantly scanning the room for any signs of movement.

I wasn't remotely prepared for what happened next.

Kayla was mid-way through a story, talking about the mirror and some of the paranormal activity surrounding it. All of a sudden, I felt a finger jab me in the small of my back.

To be absolutely clear, this wasn't my clothing shifting, my back coming into contact with some surface or object, or anything like that. This was a *jab*; solid, purposeful, and not to mention, a little bit painful.

Quite annoyed, I swung around to see what the hell Anna wanted. She was sitting in the row of seats behind me, but offset to one side by a couple of feet.

Not happy that she had broken my train of thought in such a rude way, I shot her a look that might best be described as 'the stink-eye.'

What? she mouthed back, looking puzzled.

I shook my head and went back to listening to Kayla. When her story was over and we took a five-minute break, I took Anna aside and asked her if she had been responsible for the poke.

"No," she insisted. "Why would I do something like that?"

She was right. Anna was an experienced paranormal investigator, one that I'd work alongside for several years, and while she had a great sense of humor, she was never less than one hundred percent professional while she was working. If she said that she hadn't touched me, I believed her. Ever since its inception, our team has always had a 'no pranking' policy — after all, once somebody starts playing games during a case, where does it stop? That's a slippery slope, one that, by mutual agreement, we weren't going to set foot on.

"There's something else," Anna went on. "I didn't want to interrupt Kayla while she was talking, but right before you turned around to glare at me, I was getting chills across my entire body. They were running up and down my arms, legs, and spine."

Could this have been a purely psychological phenomenon, the sort of thing that might be subconsciously caused by the knowledge that she was sitting in the cellar of one of Gettysburg's most haunted buildings, which just so happened to be decorated in the style of a Victorian-era funeral parlor?

"This wasn't my imagination, I wasn't getting spooked, and it wasn't cold air or anything like that," Anna insisted. "I had gooseflesh going on, and the hairs on the backs of my arms were all standing up on end."

For the paranormal investigator, much of the so-called 'evidence' that we gather is experiential in nature — and therefore, highly subjective. Feeling cold, numb, tingly, or one of a hundred other different sensations, while visiting a haunted location is pretty much par for the course. When they happen to just one person, these strange feelings can sometimes be written off as being little more than one's subconscious becoming a little hyper-active. Yet in our case, there were not one but *two* witnesses, each of whom experienced an odd physical effect right at the same time.

It's a little harder to dismiss that out of hand.

"So, what do you want to try next?" Jason asked. I thought about it for a moment.

"Whatever or whoever is down here, I seem to have already drawn its attention," I said at last. "Maybe we should capitalize on that."

"Capitalize how?"

"Let's see how it reacts when I'm all alone down here. You two, head on upstairs and shut me in."

This wasn't bravado on my part. A good paranormal investigator will do anything that he or she can — within reason, of course — to stimulate activity. I had been singled out for a poke in the back. Now, I was basically offering myself up as bait, in the hopes that whichever entity had interacted with me once already would be even more willing to do so when it had me all to itself.

If Anna had gotten touched, she would be the one sitting all alone in the hot seat. The same went for Jason, who, in what had seemed a bit like a farcical scene from *The Benny Hill Show*, had gotten slapped on top of his bald head at the Molly Brown House Museum in Denver.

"Good luck, man," he offered, before he and Anna walked out, closing the heavy door behind them with a thud. I could just about hear their footsteps receding up the staircase to street level. I looked around the basement/funeral parlor.

I won't deny being just a *little* bit creeped out. My imagination was already in overdrive, picturing phantom soldiers lurking in every shadow. About the only thing I had going for me, I decided, was that I was English; the Brits had flirted with the idea of supporting southern independence during the Civil War — indeed, Colonel Arthur Fremantle of the Coldstream Guards had been an observer attached to General Lee's army, and was actually present at the battle. I hoped that any ghostly Confederates would be relatively well-disposed toward having an Englishman in their midst.

Time would tell. I sat down in the same spot where I had been poked, and hoped that I hadn't bitten off more than I could chew.

A little noise filtered down through the ceiling, the sound of patrons chatting to one another in the dining area above my head. I invited any spirits that may be present to please come forward and communicate with me, either by speaking or manifesting in some physical way…such as poking me again.

I began taking photographs, working without a flash in order to avoid the ubiquitous 'dust orbs' that ruined the pictures of so many paranormal investigators. Walking over to the big dress mirror, I peered into the glass. No faces stared back at me. I did my best to ignore the figure lying in the coffin next to it, a mannequin intended to add a little atmosphere to the cellar.

Nothing. It was as quiet as the grave.

Things still hadn't picked up by the time Jason and Anna came back. The atmosphere felt flat. We devoted a lot of time to the mirror, based mostly on its reputation. All of the photographs came back normal (whether with flash, or without) and none of our readings varied from their natural baselines.

Jason fished an SB-11 spirit box out of his equipment case, set it to a fast rate of sweep, and placed it on the floor in front of the mirror. The sound of static filled the cellar as the box jumped from frequency to frequency in the AM band.

"Let's kill the lights completely," I suggested. Anna obliged, reaching out to flip off the switches. The cellar was plunged into absolute darkness, and instantly felt ten times more intimidating — thank you, psyche, and 40 years of watching horror movies that were set in places that looked a lot like this cellar.

We began to call out to the spirits of the Farnsworth House again, asking them to please draw close and interact with us. Sitting there in the dark, with the sound of radio static cranked a to near-deafening volume, still couldn't even begin to approximate the terror and claustrophobia that Mr. Sweney must have felt during the two days he spent hiding in that same cellar during the battle.

Nothing meaningful came through the box. It was getting a little frustrating, if the truth be told. I had hoped that the physical contact I had experienced earlier was the start of an active time for us in the cellar. No such luck.

Bringing up my iTunes library on my phone, I started to

play some Civil War-era music — favorite marching songs from each side of the divide, such as *Battle Hymn of the Republic*, and *Dixie*. My hope was that this might stir up some happy reminiscences for any soldiers who were still around.

Anna began to get chills again, which she assured us was nothing to do with the emotional impact of the music or the darkness of the environment. I used a very high-tech method of checking for drafts — a hanging piece of paper, illuminated by a flashlight — and determined that whatever it was that was giving Anna the chills, it didn't seem to be a breeze. This was a little strange, particularly when one considered that the air in the basement felt hot and humid. It was definitely T-shirt weather outside.

A loud clanking sound caused us a bit of a start, but we quickly determined it to be nothing more than water passing through the pipes.

Still complaining of feeling cold, Anna wrapped her arms around herself. Suddenly, I was overcome by the very same sensation. It was somewhat akin to stepping into a meat locker, a feeling of intense cold that bordered upon the freezing. It affected my entire body, and before I know it, I was shivering.

"It *is* cold right here," Jason admitted, stepping up to stand next to me. Ever the skeptic, he began to trace the cold sensation to a nearby air vent. I thought that I had ruled out the possibility of a draft being the root cause for Anna's sense of cold, but this turned out to be because she was a little further away from the vent than I was, and therefore couldn't feel it as strongly. As for the piece of paper method of debunking, well...I hadn't been holding it up high enough. The vent was above us, so I had missed it on my initial check. A mystery explained, then; a lesson learned — and a little egg on my face, to remind me to be more thorough in my debunking next time.

Anna moved away from Jason and I, taking a seat on the staircase at the back of the room. Over the course of the next few minutes, both she and I saw brief flashes of light on the back wall, in the vicinity of the haunted mirror. We couldn't find a rational explanation for them. Ordinarily, I'd have gone with them being caused by car headlights, but it was still light outside, and we hadn't seen anything like that when we'd visited the cellar after dark the night before.

Suddenly, out of nowhere, came one of the most nauseating things I have ever smelled in my entire life (and as a 17-year EMT-turned-paramedic, that's really saying something). The stench smelled like extremely bad diarrhea to me; to Jason's nose, it was more like meat being cooked. I wasn't buying that for a second. The food at the Farnsworth House was always excellent. He and I were smelling two very different things, and while it's tempting to make some kind of fart joke, none of us had passed gas down in the cellar.

I could only assume that Jason was smelling food being prepared in the kitchens, with the aroma wafting through the air vent, and I was picking up on what began to smell more and more like fecal matter. Although I am by no means psychically sensitive (that I know of) was it possible that I was picking up on the odor of human waste that would have accompanied the three-day stay of Mr. Sweney and the other civilians who had sheltered down in the cellar during the battle? The house would most likely not have had indoor toilets back then, and even if it had, nobody in their right mind would have gone upstairs in the middle of a protracted firefight in order to use one. It was far more likely that they made use of more primitive toiletary arrangements in the cellar, such as buckets and pails; while not exactly sanitary, it would have been a far better option than getting shot by a stray bullet on one of the upper floors.

Paranormal phenomena can be perceived with any of the five basic senses. Ghostly smells are not at all uncommon in haunted locations, and as quickly as it had arrived, the foul stink was gone again. Anna and Jason never smelled it. Is it possible that I was simply hallucinating? Perhaps, but I consider that to be unlikely. I have never experienced anything quite like that during a paranormal investigation, either before or since.

"It's really quiet down here," Anna said. "I could use a break. Either that, or we might want to think about relocating to another part of the building."

Jason agreed.

"Let's take five," I replied. "I want to consult with the experts to see if there's anything we might have missed."

Chapter Twelve

Life and Death

After a quick break, I called somebody who was more familiar with the ghosts of the Farnsworth House than I was.

"Hello,"a gravelly voice answered. Even over the speakerphone, the broad Texas accent was instantly recognizable. "This is Barry Klinge."

One half of the renowned Klinge Brothers, the two San Antonio-based investigators who had starred in the TV series *Ghost Lab*, Barry had helped set up the experiment in which Civil War re-enactors simulated firing from the garret of the Farnsworth House, across to the Jennie Wade House, a little further up Baltimore Street. Rather than use bullets or musket balls, however, the Klinges had opted for the much-safer choice: laser beams.

"I'm in the basement of the Farnsworth House here in Gettysburg," I explained, "and apart from a couple of interesting maybes, I've got a whole bunch of nothing going on tonight. Do you maybe have a couple of pointers?"

Barry chuckled, fully aware that 90-95% of *all*

paranormal investigations turn out that same way — empty-handed. "We got the best results up in the attic, not down in the cellar," he told us, after mulling it over a little. "You've already tried playing music from that era? Okay. Then probably the best thing to do, if I were you, would be to head on up to the attic, and just BS with your crew while you're up there. No formal EVP stuff or anything like that. Just *talk*, run a recorder discreetly, and see if one of those sharpshooter boys wants to join in with the conversation."

The three of us thanked Barry for his advice, and agreed it appeared to be sound.

"One last thing before you go," Barry added. "Do you believe in coincidences?"

"Kind of," I hedged. "But investigating the paranormal has pushed my belief in them a little too far, sometimes. Why do you ask?"

"This is going to sound kinda silly, but not thirty seconds before you called, we were sitting here at home watching a stupid TV show. Somebody on the show said that if you want to figure out your cowboy name, you add together your first car and the last name of the first girl you ever kissed."

"Okaaaaay…" I had no idea where Barry was going with

this.

"Anyway, I figured out that my cowboy name would have been Bobcat Sweney. Got that? SWENEY. Then not half a minute later, you called me from the Sweney House. How strange is that?"

We laughed. Strange, yes, but nothing more than a coincidence...

...right?

We were the only people in the attic that evening.

It had begun to rain outside, and it was coming down pretty hard when we emerged from the cellar. Because of the weather, the Sunday evening ghost tours were a little sparser than those on Friday and Saturday night had been. I made no secret of being glad to have the garret all to ourselves.

Jason put the Ovilus down on the floor. It immediately came out with three meaningless words, before quieting down for a while. Anna started a voice recorder running, while I called Brad Klinge.

Despite his gruff, fierce exterior, Brad is one of the nicest guys you could wish to meet. He also has a near-encyclopedic knowledge of the Gettysburg campaign, much of it derived from his having walked the ground himself at great length.

I explained to him that the cellar had been pretty quiet for us so far that night, and related his brother's advice to us, which, he agreed, sounded like a good idea.

"Now you're up in the attic? Don't do what we did," he boomed. "The fire department turned up because we smoked that garret out with a fog machine. We were doing our laser sniper experiment, and wanted to make it as realistic as possible. Things got a little *too* realistic. Pumping in smoke, we accidentally set off all the fire alarms."

"Whoops," I laughed.

"Our buddy Steve was up in the attic, along with two Confederate sharpshooters," Brad recalled. "Although we didn't do it on purpose, the fact that Steve was black, and was basically in command of two white Confederate soldiers, may have sparked something off with any spirits in that attic."

"I can't imagine that would have gone down well with them."

"Now, there's been some debate about whether the shot that killed Jennie Wade was actually fired from the Farnsworth garret window or not." Brad was warming to his theme. "Some historians think that it could have come from another building nearby, but ballistically, Farnsworth was the better bet.

"So, our guys had a high-powered, industrial-grade laser beam for the experiment. They fired that thing through the window, and managed to put the laser *straight through* the hole that the fatal bullet had made in the door of the Jennie Wade House. So, the shot was definitely do-able.

"Aside from shooting the breeze, like Barry said, you might want to try a little Southern-slang sniper talk tonight. Talk about shooting Yankees, blowin' their heads off, that kind of thing. It's not meant to sound disrespectful; it's exactly what those sharpshooters would have been talking about when they were up here."

"Southern slang's not exactly my forte, Brad," I grinned. "I'm a Brit, remember? You guys are all pretty much rebellious colonials to me. But my investigators should be able to handle that just fine."

"I got a good laugh out of your 4th of July Facebook post." Brad was referring to a tongue-in-cheek meme that I'd posted on Independence Day, a picture of Her Majesty the Queen, along with a caption that said: *I say, the colonies are rather rowdy today!* "What you've got to remember,

Richard, is that Gettysburg happened less than a hundred years after the War of Independence. We couldn't even make it a century without fighting amongst ourselves!"

That was a sobering thought indeed.

"I prefer to think of it like a much earlier version of Brexit," I laughed, "but much better-armed."

I was hoping that all of this banter would tempt one of the spirits to join in with the fun. Anna and Jason were taking readings, checking to see whether energy in the attic was different from its normal baseline. So far, it didn't appear to be.

"I've been to the Farnsworth quite a few times," Brad went on, changing tack slightly. "Only stayed there once, but did several public ghost-hunting events there. Most of the guest rooms seem to be pretty active. I've personally heard footsteps walking around there late at night, when nobody was up and about to make them. The same was true for disembodied voices, especially back-and-forth conversations, coming from parts of the building where there were no people. Barry and I also got a few EVPs at the house, over the years."

"Good to know," I thanked him. "We really appreciate your help tonight, Brad. Any last tips before we wrap up our investigation here?"

"One. Hop onto the Internet and see if you can find the sounds of battle from that era. You know, muskets, cannon fire, horses, men screaming and yelling, that kind of thing. It may stir something up."

"I'm on it," Anna said, bringing up the YouTube app on her phone.

"Roger that. Thanks for being a part of our investigation, sir. Any parting thoughts?"

Brad paused to think about it for a second. "Remember the episode of *Ghost Lab*, where you see Barry and I walking around at night? Well, we weren't actually on the battlefield as such. The park closes at night, and you can't walk there after dark. But we were on the back side of Little Round Top, which is private land — we'd gotten the owner's permission to be there, and to film.

"I gotta tell you, the things you could hear out there at night…cannon fire, gunfire, things like that…it's definitely paranormally active. I always tell people, you have *got* to go to Gettysburg, if for no other reason than to truly understand what *heaviness* feels like. When people say that a particular place or atmosphere felt heavy, that's what Gettysburg feels like. There's no other place like it in the world."

On that note, we said our goodbyes and left Brad to enjoy the remainder of his Sunday evening, while the three of us settled down for our last EVP session at the Farnsworth House.

The sound of musketry suddenly filled the attic, volley after volley of massed gunfire, courtesy of Anna's cell phone. Horses whinnied. Men cursed and screamed, hacking at one another with swords and thrusting with bayonets. She had found an excellent video of Civil War re-enactors, one whose soundtrack perfectly suited our needs.

All three of us sat there, lost in our own thoughts, as the sounds of battle once again filled the attic of the Farnsworth House. It was a truly sobering thought to realize that in the summer of 1863, those sounds would have been happening both inside and outside the house, but in deadly earnest. The screams would have been real, dying men calling out for their mothers, rather than simulated. The pain and terror would have been equally real.

"Front rank — Ready! Aim! FIRE!"

The sounds of muskets crashing back into the shoulders of re-enactors filled the attic.

"Fix bayonets!"

"CHARGE!"

We let the sounds of the firefight go on for another five minutes, waiting for the echoes of the last volley to die away. Then we launched into another EVP session, one aimed specifically at trying to reach the Confederate soldiers.

Nothing came through on the recordings. More than a little dejected, we decided to take a break. I took my phone out of airplane mode. A text pinged up on the screen, one that made me feel as though I'd just been sucker-punched in the gut.

A friend of mine had been found dead at her home. She and I had served as firefighters and EMTs together for many years. I didn't know the circumstances yet — it was too early to say — but she had been young, and full of life. The last time I had seen her, I remembered that we had laughed about something stupid and juvenile in my office. The slowly-dawning realization that I would never see her smiling face again was heartbreaking.

Gettysburg has always been an emotional place for me. That, coupled with this unexpected piece of bad news, brought tears to my eyes. I've learned over the years, mostly from the experiences of others, that it's a bad idea to be in a haunted location when you aren't feeling one hundred percent, emotionally speaking. It can make you vulnerable to all kinds of negativity.

"I need to call my people," I said, rubbing at my eyes. I had to make sure that the EMTs and paramedics I worked with were doing okay — at least, as okay as was possible, under the circumstances. Jason and Anna elected to keep going, running another EVP session while I went back to my room to make some calls. It was late on a Sunday evening, but I knew that none of them would be sleeping.

Downstairs, in the Sara Black Room, I checked in on my friends and colleagues. From up above me, the mournful sounds of a Civil War dirge, played on a violin and coming through one of Jason's speakers, drifted down. That damn near broke me. Before I knew it, tears were running down my face, and I was glad that neither of them could hear me crying.

It was time to call it a night. My heart wasn't in it any more. Jason and Anna were their usual respectful selves, and knew enough to give me my space. They retired to their hotel rooms, glad, I suspect, of getting an early night for once.

I stretched out on the mattress, but couldn't sleep. For the next few hours I lay there with my fingers laced behind my head, just staring at the ethereal white dress at the foot of the bed. My brain was a jumble of thoughts. All three of us were running on fumes at that point, thanks to very limited sleep and far too much caffeine. My heart was sick, my mind was exhausted, but my body was wired.

The only thing I knew for sure was that I needed to clear my head. Making as little noise as I possibly could, I crept out into the hallway and through the now-silent hallway until I reached the stairs.

It was a little after midnight. The air was still warm when I stepped out into the street. I wandered aimlessly for a while, letting my feet take me wherever they wanted to go. I passed the Jennie Wade House — no phantoms were to be seen staring out of the windows — and started to climb Cemetery Hill. Although it isn't permitted to step foot on the battlefield after dark, traveling the roads is still allowed.

I continued on uphill, lost in my own thoughts. The tears had begun to dry up now, and after a while, I began to feel a sense of great peace descend on me. I stood just outside the arch of the iconic brick gatehouse which marked the entrance to Evergreen Cemetery. It looked almost exactly the same as it had at the time of the battle.

Right next to it was the Gettysburg National Cemetery.

Although I would never have dreamed of intruding on either of them after hours, I stood outside the grounds of a while, just letting myself adjust to the events of the evening. I thought about the sacrifice made by the thousands of brave lads who were buried there.

There is always a deep sense of connection with history to be had at Gettysburg — at least, I have always felt that way. Whether it was down to my fragile emotional state, or something more, I cannot say, but tonight, that feeling of being close to the events of July 1st-4th 1863 had never been stronger. I felt privileged to be here, late at night, in one of the most incredible places in the world. None other than Abraham Lincoln himself had delivered the Gettysburg Address just a short distance off to my right, and in doing so, had defined an era for all eternity.

I kept on walking to the top of Cemetery Hill, and stood at the crest, pausing to get my breath back. There wasn't a cloud in the night sky. Overhead, the stars shone brilliantly, while all around me were statues of those who had fought and, in some cases, died on this hallowed ground. Oliver Otis Howard sat on horseback, impassively surveying the ground his men had struggled valiantly to hold. Winfield Scott Hancock, one of the most fearless and capable Union generals, was also immortalized in stone. I was among giants, and it was easy to forget that these had once been flesh and blood men, with foibles, flaws, and magnificent virtues, long before the statues were put in place.

Some of them had bled on this very ground. Some had breathed their last.

Looking at those statues, some of them no more than dark shapes silhouetted against the starry night, I began to think about life, death, and the meaning of it all. My thoughts turned back to my friend, taken so unexpectedly and long before her time…as had so many of those who were buried on this hill. Amos Humiston, whose memorial Jason and I had tracked down, was just one of those interred within.

I was suddenly struck by thoughts of the never-ending circle of struggle, life, and death that human beings had dealt with since time immemorial. The notion was a strangely comforting one, though I couldn't exactly say why.

All I knew was that when I came down Cemetery Hill, long before the sun came up, my heart was at peace again. I passed the bullet-pocked wall of the Farnsworth House, and stood for a moment, looking up at the garret window, so dark and empty. The house seemed to be welcoming me back.

Our investigation of the Farnsworth House had made for a strange and fascinating journey. Hearing from those who had experienced a brush with the otherworldly within its walls had been fascinating. I had personally experienced one piece of physical phenomena that I could not find a rational explanation for: being poked in the back while in the cellar. Try as I might, I was unable to debunk it.

For me, that was enough. As far as I was concerned, there were still spirits of some sort haunting the Farnsworth House. Were we dealing with the ghost of a young boy, hit by a carriage in the street outside, who had passed away in the Sara Black Room? The souls of long-dead Confederate snipers, re-visiting and re-living one of the most intense and stressful days of their entire lives? Could Mr. Sweney, former owner of the house, have been responsible, especially when I began asking sensitive questions about his family history? A few weeks later, I would ask myself whether the team from *Kindred Spirits* hit the nail on the head when they attributed much of the paranormal activity at the Farnsworth House to the mirror?

For every question that was answered, another reared its head. I hadn't 'solved' the Farnsworth House haunting, if such a thing is indeed even possible — but I had, at least, satisfied myself of its reality.

I crawled into bed and turned out the lights, falling asleep under the watchful eye of Sara Black. Although I slept undisturbed for what was left of the night, I had no idea that, just a few hours later, the spirits of the Farnsworth House would fire one last parting shot before I left.

Chapter Thirteen

Knock Knock

Breakfast was just coming to a close by the time I came
downstairs, bleary-eyed, and wandered through into the
dining room.

Rob and Nicole, looking remarkably bright-eyed and
bushy tailed, greeted me with a cheery hello. They waved
me over, inviting me to sit down at the table next to theirs.

Sitting opposite me was a lady I didn't recognize. Rob
introduced her as Vivian, who oversaw housekeeping at the
Inn. As I would soon come to find out, she was a fountain of
knowledge when it came to the history and ghost lore of the
Farnsworth House.

We began discussing the ghost box sessions of the last
few nights. When Rob told Vivian about the young girl who
wanted to call him 'Daddy', that struck a chord with her.
Having always been interested in the ghostly side of the Inn,
Vivian had once gotten into the habit of leaving a recorder
running whenever she was cleaning a room.

One day, she was hard at work on the second floor, and

left the recorder going in the Sweney Room. Two hours later, her job done, she retrieved the device and listened to the audio playback. On that recording, speaking loud and clear, was the voice of a little girl, saying the word *Daddy*.

"Mr. Sweney had a niece named Sissy, and she died here," Vivian went on. "The poor child was only four years old. So the next day after we recorded the little girl's voice, I went back to the room and left my tablet recording again. I said, 'Okay, Sissy! If you're here, say Daddy again.'"

"And did she?" I prompted.

"The word *Jeremy* came up on the recording. He yelled, *BOYS! HUGS!* I think he was mad that Sissy was getting all the attention. But then, very faintly, there was a whispered, *Daddy*."

Rob and Nicole looked at one another, suddenly realizing what the little girl's voice meant. Was this really the spirit of Sissy, the niece of Mr. Farnsworth, trying to find the father she had lost after so many years?

Next, Rob detailed what I was beginning to think of as the running 'prick joke.' Rather than dismiss it with a laugh, however, Vivian actually found that it prompted another memory within her.

Several years before, a young blogger had come to stay

at the Farnsworth, with the intention of blogging about some of his experiences there. Along with his female partner, he had stayed at the Inn for three or four days.

After taking a ghost tour one night, he managed to get on the bad side of the tour guide. She came to Vivian the following morning, grumbling about the man's bad behavior. 'The idiot,' as she had taken to calling him, had shown the spirits of the Farnsworth no respect whatsoever; instead, he had been deliberately antagonistic, going from room to room and provoking as loudly and aggressively as he possibly could...acting, in other words, like a complete ass.

That same day, the blogger came downstairs for breakfast with an entirely different affect than he had sported the day before. Gone was the cocky swagger, replaced with — dare I say it — a rather more *haunted* manner. He looked Vivian right in the eye and, appearing rather embarrassed, told her that he had been 'a complete prick to Mr. Sweney last night.'

Mr. Sweney had not, it seemed, taken kindly to this insult. The blogger was staying in the Sara Black Room, presumably having requested one of the more active rooms at the Farnsworth, and was just stepping through the doorway when he felt himself slammed forward onto the floor. His head was slammed into the carpet, stunning him momentarily. As he tried to pull himself together and make sense of what had just taken place, a man's voice hissed a single word into his ear: *Prick.*

The man's girlfriend was sitting on the bed, and watched the whole thing happen. He seemed to undergo a period of brief paralysis, unable to move his arms or legs in the aftermath of the attack. Things rapidly went from bad to worse when she felt a pair of unseen hands grab her ankles, and begin to pull her toward the floor as well. She quite understandably freaked out, but the invisible grip was released just seconds later.

The couple fled downstairs and immediately checked out of the Farnsworth, choosing to stay with friends over an hour's drive away. Although he had returned to the inn for breakfast and to talk with some of the staff there, the man flatly refused to ever spend another night under its roof again.

"Sometimes, karma can be *very* quick," I said, while telling myself privately how glad I was that I hadn't done any provoking there at the inn. In truth, I had never even considered it anyway. The spirits of the Farnsworth House deserved my respect and my compassion, nothing less. There was no way I was going to stomp around the place, antagonizing and insulting them. My fellow investigators all felt the same way.

To give him credit, the rather abashed blogged admitted that he *had* been acting disrespectfully toward Mr. Sweney, and added that, "He called me out on it."

For his part, Rob hadn't been acting that way, as far as I could tell. The approach that he took during our ghost box session was one of relaxed, good-natured humor, but it was interesting that the P-word had once again been bestowed on a visitor to the Farnsworth House. Had the same entity been involved in both cases? It is impossible to say for sure. I, for one, would make the case that the spirit of Mr. Sweney might not be responsible in either instance. Perhaps one of the soldiers that are said to haunt the place was responsible…but then again, perhaps it *had* been the spirit of Mr. Sweney. I had no way of knowing that, just a few minutes into our interview, he would make his presence known to us all in a most unexpected way.

It wasn't long after Vivian had first begun working at the Farnsworth House, that she became convinced that the historic residence truly lived up to its haunted reputation.

It began with little things, at first; the sort of small, strange happenings that it was easy to dismiss as simply being 'just one of those things.'

Take, for example, the day she happened to be cleaning the Jeremy Room. It happened to be Mother's Day, which usually means that the Inn is a little busier than normal — and, by extension, there is extra energy around for the spirits to manipulate.

Because of its connection to the ghostly little boy that is said to haunt the Farnsworth House, the Jeremy Room contains a number of toys for his spirit to play with. A number of blocks, each inscribed with letters, are stacked on a shelf in one part of the room. Some guests hope that Jeremy will use the blocks to spell out a word, giving some sign of his presence.

There is also a blue plastic ball, which is said to sometimes take on a life of its own. When Vivian had finished dusting, she set the ball down carefully in the middle of the shelf, and placed the blocks on all sides, completely fencing it in.

"Okay, Jeremy…if you want to play, I have a few minutes. Go right ahead…"

As if on cue, the ball hopped up and over the blocks, fell to the floor, and bounced.

Suitably impressed, Vivian chased the ball down, and placed it right back in the center of the blocks.

"If that really was you, Jeremy, let's see if you can do that again."

The ball immediately obliged, leaping over the blocks once more, and diving to the floor like a particularly enthusiastic lemming.

Suitably impressed, Vivian nonetheless wanted to see if it would happen again. "Third time's the charm," she called out, returning the ball to its place on the shelf one last time. No sooner had she done so and stepped back, than the ball was rolling across the floor again, meandering in the general direction of the door.

She soon came to realize that the Jeremy Room is one of the Farnsworth's more active rooms. On more than one occasion, she would be walking past, on her way to do something else, and would hear a great commotion going on inside there. Whenever she opened the door to take a look inside, everything was quiet and peaceful. Despite the fact that the room was always totally empty, every single one of those toy blocks would be laying on the floor, as if a child had just been playing with them.

There seems to be a definite element of the prankster where Jeremy is concerned. He has earned himself a reputation for knocking repeatedly on the door of his room while it is being cleaned and made over. Whenever the staff member in question opens the door to take a look, there is never anybody standing out there in the hallway.

After her first encounter with the ghost of Jeremy, Vivian didn't need any more convincing that the Farnsworth House was haunted. Yet over the course of her years working there, guest after guest have approached her and told her of their own paranormal experiences while staying at the inn. After having heard so many, she is now a veritable walking repository of Farnsworth ghost stories — some of which are more memorable than others.

Take, for example, the case of the couple from Michigan, who had booked their stay at the Farnsworth in order to celebrate her graduation from nursing school. During their five day stay, the couple spent two nights in the Sara Black Room, two nights in the Jeremy Room, and their final night in the McFarlane room. An avowed enthusiast when it came to all things paranormal, the newly-graduated nurse had brought her own ghost hunting equipment along with her.

Just as they were checking out to leave, she excitedly beckoned Vivian over to see her. "You have *got* to take a look at this," the nurse gushed. 'This' turned out to be a piece of footage from a video camera that had been positioned near the doorway of the McFarlane Room, its field of vision covering the bed and the wall alongside it. Hanging from that wall is a small child's dress, Victorian in style and more than a little creepy (I vividly remember waking up in that room at some ungodly hour of the morning and getting the shock of my life, thinking that the dress was floating in the darkness right there in front of me!)

"Watch the dress," the nurse said. Vivian kept her eye on it. The dress seemed to be overlaid with a strange blue light, something which she had never seen in that room before. It looked like a backward letter L.

All of a sudden, the dress flipped itself up into the air, then dropped back down again. It was as if an unseen hand had given it an almighty push. At first, it might be tempting to suspect that a gust of wind was responsible, but the windows were closed and there were no air vents in the area from which any sort of breeze could have originated.

"That's impressive,' she had been forced to admit.

"That's not all. Just wait." The nurse fast-forwarded to a few hours later. Now it was the following morning, as evidenced by the bright daylight streaming through the windows. Her husband was still fast asleep, but she was waking up and getting out of bed.

Vivian watched as she went into the bathroom and closed the door behind her. Five minutes passed without incident. Then Vivian looked closer, and saw that the same, strange light pattern — the reversed L-shape — was back, but this time, it was superimposed over the bathroom door knob…

…which began to turn, all by itself. It was as if an invisible hand had grasped it and was starting to twist. The door popped open, showing a sliver of light from within the bathroom.

The nurse had gotten a little more than she had bargained for, when she checked herself and her husband into the McFarlane Room!

Nor was that the only story relating to the room I had spent two nights in. Just two weeks before our interview, Vivian had spoken with a different guest, one who was also intrigued by the Farnsworth's ghost stories, and had therefore requested a haunted room. Just like the newly-graduated nurse, this guest had also set up a video camera and left it running inside the McFarlane Room. She claimed to have captured on video the apparition of an older man, sitting in the chair by the side of the bed.

This tracks with the eyewitness testimony of previous guests, several of whom have claimed to see the mournful figure of just such a man, sitting in exactly the same place. Although I could find no historical evidence to support it, Farnsworth House lore contends that this is the forlorn figure of Jeremy's bereaved father, still mourning the death of his son more than one hundred years after he died in the bathroom of the Sara Black Room.

If so, I find this to be unbelievably tragic. Assuming, for a moment, that both Jeremy and his father not only each haunt the Farnsworth, then how awful would it be for them to both be unaware of one another's presence? Those who encounter this gentleman all describe him similarly — he is said to wear period clothing, and always looks disconsolate and downcast. Jeremy is an intelligent spirit, one that seems only too happy to interact with the living guests and staff at the inn. His father, on the other hand (if that really is the identity of the male apparition) does not seem to be interactive at all, which implies that he is a residual apparition. One can only hope that is really the case, for the thought of this poor man's spirit still being wracked with remorse and guilt after so many years, especially with the spirit of his son quite happily roaming the rooms and corridors of the Farnsworth House without a care in the world, is a sad thing to contemplate.

There is some debate as to whether Jeremy existed at all, let alone whether he died in the house. Vivian told me that Jeremy lived a few blocks away, was hit by a carriage or buggy in the street outside, and was carried into what is now the Sara Black Room, where he subsequently died in the nursery (now the bathroom).

"He supposedly died in his father's arms, while his father was sitting in a rocking chair," she claims. During our interview, I asked Vivian politely about the validity of the historical record. "It was investigated when Mr. and Mrs. Schultz bought the place, by their daughter, Patti O'Day, who was a sensitive. After moving in, Patti began to have some extremely vivid dreams about the house.

(Some of Patti's insights and stories concerning the haunting of the Farnsworth House Inn have been collected in the book *Gettysburg's Haunted Address: Spirits of Farnsworth House Inn*, by Bernadette Loeffel-Atkins. The book is somewhat difficult to find at the time of writing, but is well worth the read if you can track down a copy).

I would like to point out that we have Ms. O'Day to thank for gathering and sharing many of the Farnsworth House Inn ghost stories, often telling them to tourists and visitors in the basement mourning theater. Nobody can write about the haunting of this grand old Gettysburg landmark without offering their respects to her — thank you for enshrining the ghosts of the old Sweney House in the haunted history books, Ma'am! (Unfortunately, I was unable to get in touch with her during the research and writing of this book).

Taking up the story once more, Vivian told me that after Patti began to have psychic experiences inside the house, she invited in a medium to help shed some light on those events. The medium picked up on the spirit of a young boy, one who was crying and upset because he didn't want to leave.

"His name is Jeremy," the medium said, "and he insists that he will not leave this house, because he is happy here."

Although the Farnsworth is perhaps best known for stories about Civil War soldiers haunting the place, Jeremy is by far the most active spirit there, Vivian says. This tracks with what I was told by other members of the housekeeping staff, all of whom confirmed that Jeremy was the mischievous little specter that they encountered most often while making up rooms.

Yet there are other phenomena too. Residents of the Schultz and Eisenhower Rooms sometimes report hearing the sound of bugles and gunshots, most likely residual auditory phenomena that date back to the days of the battle itself. In addition to the attic, dragging sounds have also been heard coming from a number of the guest rooms, as though something heavy was being moved across the floorboards.

Somewhat less pleasant is the sudden, unexplained sulfurous stench which also permeates the Schultz and Eisenhower rooms from time to time. Some have also described it as being akin to a 'rotting smell.' While it would be easy to write this off as being a sanitation issue, there is never anything wrong with the plumbing or nearby sewers whenever they are checked. We must bear in mind that paranormal phenomena can be detected by all five of our normal senses, including the sense of smell, and it is entirely possible that what people are smelling is actually a throwback to July of 1863, when the stink of gunpowder would have filled the house from floor to rafters. And as for the rotting smell, well...

One day, Vivian and a colleague named Barbara were in the part of the inn dedicated to housekeeping. They were folding a bed sheet as neatly as possible. The two women chatted, raising their voices a little to be heard over the sound of the dryer, which kept up a steady background rumble.

Suddenly, apropos of nothing, the dryer door flew open, as if yanked by an invisible hand, and then slammed shut again. The machine reverberated with a loud, metallic clang. Barbara looked at Vivian in a manner that seemed to say, *Did that really just happen?* She was relatively new to the Farnsworth House at that time, and this incident was to be her first brush with the resident spirits.

Needless to say, it would not be her last.

One of the more common occurrences at the Farnsworth happens in the Jennie Wade Room, which is one of the newer guest rooms, located in the garden area, away from the main house. Vivian ranks the Jennie Wade Room as being the most paranormally-active room in the more modern part of the Inn.

"Somebody did a Ouija board session in there," she said, shaking her head. "We don't allow them to be done here.

People say that they're portals."

Vivian is referring to the theory that talking boards, as they are more generically known, are capable of opening up inter-dimensional doorways — portals — that can allow spirit entities to pass back and forth between their plane of existence and our own. Needless to say, not all of those entities are going to be nice…

Few aspects of paranormal research are more divisive and contentious than the talking board. Over the course of my career as a paranormal investigator, I have been fortunate enough to speak with people on all sides of this particularly debate. Some insist that, if used properly, the board is no more dangerous than a ghost box, or any other means of spirit communication; others, however, give dire warnings against ever allowing such a board to be used, citing examples in which negative entities are said to have come through, and wreaked havoc on the lives of the participants.

The true answer, I have come to believe, lies somewhere in the middle. A talking board is a tool, and all tools have some capacity for causing harm if they are misused. The same is true of a car, an axe, or thousands of other objects in everyday use. As long as the participants clearly express that they will *only* work with good, decent, well-meaning spirits, and remember to close the board down properly afterward ('shutting the door') then such sessions are usually quite safe. Of course, this is just my opinion, and I have been known to be wrong before...

At any rate, spirit boards are not welcome at the Farnsworth, and although I had brought one with me, I deferred to the wishes of the owners and left it in the car. I would just have to see what I could find out without making use of this one particular method. That didn't bother me one bit. There were plenty more tools in my kit.

I asked Vivian to elaborate on what ghostly phenomena had been reported from the Jennie Wade Room. An invisible cat has been heard in there quite often. Nor does the phantom feline confine itself to Wade; guests in the McFarlane Room have felt it kneading them in the middle of the night, and the sound of meowing is also sometimes heard outside the doors of the Sara Black and Sweney Rooms. Needless to say, the Farnsworth House does not have a living, flesh and blood cat living on the premises.

Inside the Jennie Wade Room, a heavy, thick rug covers the floor in front of a comfortable settee. Vivian is very particular about how she likes the rooms to be set up. Whenever the room is being prepared for new guests, she insists upon the rug being pulled out from underneath the settee's wooden legs. The housekeeping staff are diligent about making sure this happens — yet as regular as clockwork, whenever they go back into the room after having done so, they find the rug tucked in underneath the piece of furniture once more. It is almost as if somebody wants to defy Vivian's wishes regarding the layout of the room.

The guests who had used the talking board had abandoned it when they checked out, leaving it — and any negative consequences — for the staff to deal with. There was nothing special about this particular board; it was just the standard cardboard model, the kind that can be bought for less than $20 online. But Vivian couldn't help worrying about what might have come through the doorway that it represented.

Speaking of doorways: in the aftermath of the unsanctioned talking board session, the door to the Jennie Wade Room began to open all by itself. Staff members would be walking in the area, and find the door standing ajar, leaving the room open for just anybody to randomly wander in from the street outside.

If this had taken place just once or twice, it would be

easy to dismiss out of hand, attributing it to nothing more than a forgetful guest or staff member neglecting to close the door after leaving the room. But when Vivian began to lose count of the number of times it had happened, she was finally forced to admit that something otherworldly was at work. Staff members and guests alike all swore that they had closed *and locked* the door behind them, prior to it being found standing open again just a short time later.

After several guests reported experiencing strange events in the Jennie Wade Room, it was finally decided that enough was enough. Vivian brought in somebody to conduct a cleansing ceremony on the Jennie Wade Room. Things seem to have quieted down in there since then, although guests must bear in mind that where the Farnsworth House is concerned, 'quieted down' is a very relative term...

"It happened to a friend of ours just a couple of nights ago, on Friday night," Nicole chimed in. "He was staying in the Jennie Wade Room, and he's one hundred percent sure that he locked the door behind him when he went out. When he came back, the room was wide open."

Cleansings are all well and good, I thought to myself. *But your mileage may vary...*

I found it fascinating to note that the Jennie Wade

Room, and those which surrounded it, were built during the 1970s, long after the Sweney House was constructed, and over a century after the battle had taken place. Once again, as far as I was concerned, this proved the time-honored theory that said: It's not the house, it's the *land* it was built on. Despite the fact that these rooms were relatively new in comparison to the main building, they were built upon ground that had once been soaked in the blood, the site of intense emotion and great trauma. While the guests making use of the talking board in the Jennie Wade Room might have exacerbated things, I suspected that these rooms would have been haunted since day one, no matter what. Their very foundations were steeped in the events and energies of July 1863.

"Mr. and Mrs. Schulz saved this place," Vivian went on, warming to her theme. "Mr. Schulz is a huge history buff, you see. When they bought the house, it was under threat of being demolished and having a convenience store or a gas station built on the site. He promised the Gideon-Black family, who had owned the place, that he would work to restore it to its former glory."

The Shulzes had plainly been true to their word, I thought, looking around the room at the beautiful wood furnishings and elegant decor. Crossing the threshold of the Farnsworth House Inn these days, really feels as though one has stepped back in time. As the four of us talked the morning away, the strains of Civil War-era tunes formed the backdrop to our conversation, discreetly piped in over a small speaker system. With the windows closed, if one could just mentally tune out the sound of the traffic on Baltimore Street outside, it really was easy to believe that this was 1863 once more. Just the mere thought of this beautiful house being torn apart and replaced with a 7/11 made my guts churn, and I wondered whether the public knew and appreciated what a monumental debt of gratitude they owed to Mr. and Mrs. Schulz for preserving this crucial part of Gettysburg's heritage.

I asked what Mr. and Mrs. Schulz thought of the Farnsworth House's ghostly reputation. Vivian smiled and told me about the time that Mrs. Schulz's sister encountered an apparition in the tavern. She was waiting for a delivery early one morning, when she happened to look up and out of the window. There, as plain as day, she saw a man in a Confederate uniform standing there by the fish pond, looking right back at her.

What with this being the town of Gettysburg, it was

entirely possible that the man in gray was nothing more than a re-enactor, out for an early morning stroll — perhaps a little unlikely, at six o'clock in the morning, but still possible...

...and that remained a possibility, right up to the point at which he walked forward, passed through one of the walls, and disappeared.

When she had first started cooking at the Farnsworth, she hadn't believed in ghosts. Now, she saw things in an entirely different light.

Such stories are the bread and butter of life at the inn, and I couldn't help but wonder aloud whether they had problems keeping staff because of the paranormal activity. Indeed, I have worked on a number of cases in the past where the livelihood of a business was jeopardized by the ghostly goings-on. Vivian assured me that things were entirely different at the Farnsworth House, where the people who worked there actually rather enjoyed it when things began to get a little strange. As many of them saw it, it was all part of the character of the place, and the ghosts were very much a part of the family — something to be celebrated, rather than feared.

Although some visiting guests may find the phenomena

frightening, the truth is that this is primarily a friendly haunting…for the most part. Still, every once in a while, even the staff find things to be a little bit spooky. Over the winter holidays, for example, things slow down considerably. Gettysburg has fewer visitors at that time of year, which translates to fewer guests staying at the Farnsworth. On some days, there are no visitors at all. Those are the days on which the housekeeping team conducts a deep clean on the house, detailing every single fixture and fitting.

Even when the kitchen is completely shut down, the sounds of pots and pans rattling can be heard coming from that empty part of the building, along with the sounds of drawers and doors opening and closing themselves. Most staff members quickly decide that discretion is the better part of valor, and tend to leave the ghosts to their own devices.

I have always been fascinated with the concept of cyclical hauntings. These are cases which center around a specific time of the year, usually one during which a momentous event occurred. Paranormal activity in a haunted location can often build up in the weeks and days running up to the anniversary, peak around the time of the event, and then slowly begin to fall off.

Such is the case with the Grenadier, one of London's most haunted pubs. It is one of the British capital's best-kept open secrets, a delightful little historic drinking establishment right in the heart of Belgravia, one of central London's most moneyed and opulent neighborhoods. Legend has it that the Grenadier was once the officer's mess of a regiment of British infantry soldiers during the Napoleonic Wars, and was often said to be frequented by none other than the Duke of Wellington himself. A young officer, having run up heavy gambling debts and then subsequently accused of cheating at cards, was supposedly beaten to death by his comrades for this most ungentlemanly behavior, and breathed his last in what is now the public house located on Wilton Mews.

With such a gruesome past, it should therefore come as no surprise to find out that the Grenadier has long had the reputation for being haunted by the spirit of the tragic soldier. As a young lad growing up in England, I had read about the pub in the books of the great British ghost hunter, Peter Underwood, who had said that phenomena such as phantom footsteps, strange odors, and bizarre light anomalies have been reported for many years, and seem to grow more frequent and intense as the date of the young soldier's murder approaches. Finally, once that dreadful anniversary has passed, things return to normal around the Grenadier once more...only for the cycle to start up all over again the following year.

I always drop into the Grenadier for a pint of Spitfire Ale whenever I'm in London, and I encourage you to do so as well. On my last visit, the bartender kindly offered to take me down into the cellar, where some of the strongest paranormal activity is said to take place. If you're sitting at the bar, nursing a drink, and happen to look up, you'll noticed hundreds of bank notes stuck to the ceiling. These come from many countries all around the world, each one left by a well-wisher who wants to help the tortured soul of the infantry officer pay off his gambling debts, for legend has it that only when his account is paid in full can the poor lad's soul finally rest in peace.

Although these two historic locations are thousands of miles apart, the parallels between them both were not lost on me. Both had an obvious military connection, of course. Both of them had been the scene of a bloody confrontation, although the scale of death that occurred in and around the Farnsworth House was far greater than anything that happened at the Grenadier. But most fascinating of all, we have the story of the Grenadier haunting building up to its apex at the time of the murder. Did activity at the Farnsworth House build in a similar manner throughout the spring and summer months, reaching maximum effect in July, then beginning to decline? I put this question to Vivian. Her answer surprised me.

"It used to be that way," she confirmed. "Things got very heavy around the 4th of July. But over the past few years, that's changed. Now, we don't see it as much. It's been really quiet, in fact."

Paranormally speaking, things might be quiet, but Gettysburg is never busier than the 4th of July weekend. I wondered whether there was so much hustle and bustle going on in the town around that time of year, that people simply weren't noticing the strange things going on. Then again, that massive influx of visitors to the town (and therefore to the Farnsworth) ought to bring with it a lot of potential energy that the spirits should be able to use, if it suited their purpose. Was it simply a case of them wanting to lay low when there were so many new people around, especially when a significant number of them came to Gettysburg with one goal in mind — to hunt ghosts?

I took another sip of my tea, and listened with great interest as Vivian began telling me all about a dress that her daughter had purchased. It was an old dress, and almost certainly came with a lot of history attached.

Part-way through the story, we all paused and looked up. From a cabinet that stood behind Vivian, only a few feet away, there had come a very loud knock.

"That's odd," I said, craning my neck to look over her shoulder. "There's nobody back there."

The knock had been clear and distinct, and I could see nothing obvious to explain it. It wasn't the sort of sound made by pipes banging as water passed through them. This was the noise made by something solid knocking on wood, and what was more, it had originated *inside* the sealed cabinet.

"If somebody did that," I called out into thin air, "Could you please do it again?"

Other than the sounds of a melancholy Civil War dirge coming through the speakers, there was silence.

Vivian picked up the story where she had left off, relating some strange happenings that had begun as soon as her daughter had purchased the dress, which dated back to the 1800s. The tale was a sad and fascinating one. A sensitive who had been consulted on the case had told Vivian's daughter that the dress had indeed come with a spirit attachment, in the form of a heartbroken young man. The dress, she said, had been made for a young lady by her mother. Tragically, the young woman had died of respiratory failure, and now her grief-stricken beau followed it around wherever it went. Although she didn't lack sympathy for her uninvited phantom houseguest, Vivian's daughter quite understandably wanted him gone, and felt she had no choice but to have her home cleansed in order to remove the attachment.

"The only way to make this stop is to get rid of the dress," the psychic instructed her, so Vivian's daughter ended up sending it to a re-enactor in Virginia.

From the instant the dress had left her house, the ghostly activity immediately stopped.

A few weeks later, she got a call from the re-enactor, who sounded more than a little freaked out.

"There's something wrong with this dress — every time I hang it up in the closet, I come back to find it laid out on my bed when I get home! I want the thing gone!"

Although it was the last thing in the world she wanted to do, Vivian's daughter nevertheless accepted the dress back.

Listening intently as Vivian spoke, we all kept our eyes on the cabinet, practically daring another knock to take place.

KNOCK.

I sat bolt upright. Once again, it had come from inside the cabinet. Not only had we all heard it, but it had been picked up by my digital voice recorder as well. I went over to take a closer look at the cabinet. There was nothing out of place. Nothing had moved inside it. So, what had been responsible for the sound?

Stumped for an explanation, I returned to my seat. Conversation resumed, the topic shifting to the Sweney family and their history with the house. As is mentioned elsewhere in this book, while entire families sheltered in their cellars during the battle of Gettysburg, only Mr. Sweney himself (along with some others, who were not related) took cover in the cellar of the Farnsworth House. His wife and children lived elsewhere in town, something that seemed rather strange to me, all things considered.

As things turned out, all had not been well with the Sweney marriage. They had actually been separated at the time of the battle — something almost unheard of during the 1860s, when marriage was believed to be for life. Quoted in the excellent book *In the Eye of the Storm: The Farnsworth House and the Battle of Gettysburg*, by Timothy H. Smith (published 2008 by Farnsworth Military Impressions) is a letter from James Sweney to his mother. In it, Mr. & Mrs. Sweney's son alludes to potential mistreatment of his sister, Elizabeth, by her father, Harvey Sweney. While the nature of this alleged mistreatment is unclear, we can say for certain that Mrs. Sweney and at least some of the children were estranged from their father at the time of the battle.

While we were discussing this rather delicate subject in discreetly hushed tones, there came an unexpected clattering noise from my right. We all looked in that direction, to see the heavy blinds swaying back and forth in front of the window. Something appeared to have struck them. There was no breeze or draft coming through the room at the time, and none of us were within arm's length of them. It had sounded as though somebody had given them a smack.

I gave the window a closer look. Nobody had been passing outside and nobody had touched the window itself…so what had struck the blinds?

"Do you think that was a coincidence?" I asked Vivian, shooting her a sideways glance. She shook her head.

"No. I think Mr. Sweney's probably mad at me right now, for talking about this with you."

In order to deflect his ire, we quickly changed the subject. Vivian's eleven year-old grand-daughter, Faith, had joined us. She wasn't a big fan of the Farnsworth House much of the time, finding it 'pretty creepy,' but she sometimes helped her grandmother around the place. She told us very solemnly that a few days before, she had been upstairs in the Sara Black Room, and had heard the sound of children giggling, coming from somewhere out in the hallway.

"That really creeped me out," she admitted.

"It would have creeped me out too," I agreed, especially given the fact that the Sara Black Room had been my bedroom for the past couple of nights.

On that note, I shook hands with everybody, and went to check out. It was time for Jason, Anna, and I to hit the road. My final thought was that one day, in the not-so-distant future, I would return to the Farnsworth House again. So much of its story remained untold.

Once the house gets into your blood, it tends to draw you back to it, as so many guests and staff members had told me during our interviews.

Until then, dear reader, the Farnsworth will do what it has always done: keep a close hold of its mysteries, and offer the warmest of welcomes to those who come to call.

Just remember to be respectful…

Chapter Fourteen

"Our Headquarters!"

Originally, the chapter that you have just read is where I intended to finish this book.

Life, as is so often the case, had other ideas.

I'm used to having the last word when I write about a haunted location, but in this case, that privilege went to somebody far more worthy.

The last word on the Farnsworth House is going to none other than Major General Winfield Scott Hancock himself.

For those who heed its calling, the study of Civil War history involves far more than memorizing dates, places, events, and battles. Yes, it is about all of those things, but above all else, the personalities of the era stand out.

When it comes to the story of the Gettysburg campaign, some of those names shine very brightly indeed — names such as Lee, Longstreet, Chamberlain…and Hancock.

General Winfield Scott Hancock was a truly remarkable

man. Born in 1824, Hancock was awarded a place at the U.S. Military Academy, West Point, sixteen years later. Surprisingly, he proved to be a less-than-stellar student, graduating nowhere near the top of his class. There were few indications that he would go on to serve his nation with great distinction twenty years later — and earn himself the soubriquet, 'Hancock the Superb.'

Hancock served under General Winfield Scott during the Mexican War. His parents had named him after the general, so there was a certain synchronicity to this particular posting. It was in Mexico that Hancock first saw the face of battle in all its raw ugliness, and also suffered a wound whose after-effects would prevent him from being present at the moment of final victory.

1861 brought civil war, and saw Hancock stationed on the west coast, in California. During this time, he had become firm friends with a number of fellow army officers, who, tragically, he would end up facing on the opposite side of the battle-line at Gettysburg. One, the steadfast and pious Lewis Armistead (ironically nicknamed 'Lo' or 'Lothario' by his men, a gentle jab at Armistead's utter devotion to his wife) would become a true confidante and brother.

Starting out as a captain, Hancock's rise through the

ranks of the Union Army was nothing short of meteoric, something not particularly unusual during time of war — after all, many of the army's finest officers had followed the call of their conscience, and departed its ranks in order to serve the Southern cause. That left a number of command billets to be filled at all levels.

Some appointments and promotions were unabashedly political, with commands being doled out to those who had the right connections. This never applied to Hancock, who developed a reputation for being a competent commander and outstanding tactician purely upon his own merits. He kept a cool head when under fire, and cared as much for the welfare of his troops as for his own safety — yet never at the expense of accomplishing the mission.

His continued success earned him the rank of Major General, and with it, a division of his own. More major engagements — including bloodbaths at Chancellorsville and Fredricksburg — cost him more wounds, but his richly deserved reputation as a true 'fighting general' also earned him command of the Army of the Potomac's II Corps.

Then came Gettysburg.

On the first day of the battle, Brigadier General John Buford and his blocking force of cavalrymen had one task:

to snarl up the Confederate advance long enough for reinforcements to arrive. This they did with great gusto, forming consecutive lines of battle upon the ridges along the northern and western sides of Gettysburg. The horse soldiers soaked up each Confederate attack, blunting its momentum, making it stall, and then falling back to a fresh line of defense.

As the day wore on, those reinforcements finally came in the form of Major General John Reynolds, riding at the head of his I Corps. Reynolds was more than a Corps commander, though, because the head of the Army of the Potomac, George Meade, had given him commander of an entire wing. Reynolds was bringing more than 30,000 men to Gettysburg, and they were ready for a fight.

The fighting was particularly fierce at a place called Herbst Woods, where Reynolds found himself in the thick of it. The general's head snapped backwards as a bullet ripped into his neck. Reynolds fell from his horse and lay motionless on the ground while the battle raged all around him.

General Meade could hardly believe it when he received word of his subordinate's death. He needed somebody to take over the left wing of the army, and quickly. As he saw it, there were few suitable candidates who were capable enough to be entrusted with the job. Although there were other, more senior officers on the field, one name sprang to the forefront: Hancock. Meade immediately dispatched him to the battlefield, with orders to assume command of the forces in the field and provide him with an accurate appraisal of the tactical situation on the ground.

Meade had given Hancock the latitude to execute a fighting withdrawal from Gettysburg, if he judged it prudent to do so. One look at the terrain, and the respective battle formations of the two armies, told Hancock all that he needed to know. This was good ground on which to make a stand.

Hancock elected to stay and fight. He can therefore rightly be described as the man who guaranteed that a major battle would take place at Gettysburg. Had he chosen otherwise, the Army of the Potomac would have fallen back to a position of Meade's choosing, with the intention of fighting Lee at another place and another time. His men fell back upon Cemetery Hill, where infantry and artillery positions would form a bulwark upon which the retreating Union forces could rally and re-form. Hancock's calming influence soothed frazzled nerves, and helped restore a sense of equilibrium to units that had all but fled from their enemies.

The second day saw Hancock at the center of the Union line, commanding the entire southern half of the battlefield. Robert E. Lee, commanding the Army of Northern Virginia, hurled furious assaults against Meade's left and right. Although the center saw less fighting, that which did occur was nothing short of ferocious.

Hancock prowled back and forth on Cemetery Ridge, directing the battle with a keen and practiced eye. Further south, a bloodbath was taking place in the Peach Orchard, thanks to the arrogance of Union general Daniel Sickles. Unhappy with the terrain he had been instructed to hold, Sickles had instead pushed his troops too far forward, seeking to seize and hold what he believed to be better ground. His men would pay dearly for his hubris. Sickles's over-extended line formed a salient, bulging outward from the main line of defense and all but begging the enemy to smash it. This they promptly did, pummeling the beleaguered Federals from multiple sides.

Before anybody knew what was going on, the southern sector of the Union line was in danger of collapse. Now was the time for the Confederates to press their advantage, sending in a fresh wave of attackers against their opponents on Cemetery Ridge.

Fortunately, Hancock was there to steady the line. Ever-present where the fighting was fiercest, his natural air of authority buoyed his men's spirits in the face of almost overwhelming enemy numbers. The boys in blue kept their nerve, trading shots with the lads in butternut and resolutely holding their ground. Hancock had positioned his troops precisely where he wanted them, using the terrain to their best advantage.

Confederate brigade after brigade assaulted the Union center, inexorably grinding the defenders down and beating them back. Suddenly, Hancock found himself in the middle of a crisis. A gray tide was rushing toward him, and his section of Cemetery Ridge was sparsely defended.

He saw what was coming next: breakthrough, and inevitable collapse.

Hancock spurred his horse toward the closest friendly unit, which numbered just 262 men. They identified themselves as the 1st Minnesota, a name that would become infamous in the annals of Civil War combat, because their lives were about to be sacrificed in order for Hancock to buy the time he so desperately needed to organize a hasty defense.

The boys from Minnesota were tired but still had plenty of fight left in them. Hancock took their commanding officer, Colonel William Colvill Jr, aside, and pointed toward the mass of enemy troops now heading their way. Above the advancing enemy line fluttered a battle flag. Hancock ordered Colvill to get over there and take that flag from the Confederates.

One can only imagine what Colvill and his men thought of that order. They must certainly have known that Hancock was sending them to their deaths. But their response was to obey, and the small cluster of Minnesotans fixed bayonets and stormed the enemy formation. Although they checked the advance of the men from Alabama, the 1st Minnesota paid a terrible price. Confederates swarmed around them on all sides, hurling a storm of lead into their already-ragged ranks.

By the time the desperate encounter was over, the Minnesotans had lost more than eighty percent of their fighting strength, to death or severe wounding. It was the highest percentage of battlefield casualties taken by a unit at Gettysburg on either side, and the second largest loss *ever* inflicted upon any American unit in a single day's action (in which the unit in question ultimately survived).

Hancock must have felt himself to be a butcher, sending so many brave young men to such a gruesome fate. And yet, he had done his duty, just as the Minnesotans had done theirs. The hopelessly heroic assault of the First Minnesota had plugged a crucial gap in his lines, which were stretched perilously thin — but still they held.

When the smoke cleared, forty-seven men straggled back to the Union lines to rejoin Hancock. Their valiant last stand had taken just twenty minutes. It would be easy to believe that this would have cut the heart out of the survivors, but the men from Minnesota were made of hardy stuff indeed; the following day, July 3, would see them once again standing in the Union battle line, helping to repel the massed Confederate assault known as Pickett's Charge.

Pickett's Charge was preceded by an earth-shattering cannonade. Practically every gun that the Confederates could bring to bear was focused upon the Union line. The thunderous barrage was heard as far away as Baltimore. Chancing everything on one last throw of the dice, Robert E. Lee launched his remaining infantry brigades against the Union center on Cemetery Ridge. Lee had attacked both the enemy left and right on the preceding day. It was impossible for an army to be strong *everywhere,* Lee reasoned, and therefore, Meade's center was probably the most vulnerable point. One single, overwhelming blow there might be decisive, if luck was with them.

Luck was not with them. Meade had shifted some units around overnight, reinforcing his center and bolstering the units on Cemetery Ridge. The massed cannonade was surprisingly ineffective, doing little to soften up the defensive position that Pickett and his troops were ordered to attack.

Despite the fact that it made him a highly visible target, Hancock declined to dismount from his horse. Once again, he was to be found where the lead flew thickest, encouraging his men to stand their ground, come what may.

When a worried subordinate expressed concern for what he believed to be undue risk that Hancock was taking, he waved the man's concerns away with a disdainful, "There are times when a corps commander's life does not count."

Predictably, a general on horseback was too tempting for Confederate soldiers to resist taking potshots at. Whether aimed or a stray, we will never know, but one bullet ricocheted from Hancock's saddle and punched into the inside of his right thigh. Blood gushed from the open wound.

Hancock's aides helped him out of the saddle and laid him gently on the ground. Seeing that the bleeding was life-threatening, one officer applied a leather strap distal to the wound, acting as a tourniquet. It staunched the blood flow enough to save Hancock's life.

Along with the shot itself, a saddle nail and several slivers of wood had also been driven into the wound. Hancock personally dug the nail out of his own leg, and even found the strength to make a joke about it.

Nobody could have blamed him if he had immediately turned over command to another qualified officer and allowed himself to be taken to the closest field hospital. Winfield Scott Hancock, however, was not that sort of man. He insisted upon staying put on the field, giving orders and directing his portion of the battle until events had been decided to his satisfaction. Only then did he permit himself to seek medical treatment.

After the battle was over, Hancock stayed in the fight for the long haul, serving as a general until the very end of the war. The wound he had sustained on Cemetery Ridge may have slowed him down, but it couldn't stop him from doing what he did best.

The death of President Abraham Lincoln came as a

shock to the people of the United States, Hancock included. The assassins were duly captured, arraigned, and sentenced. In what he found to be a rather distasteful assignment, Hancock was ordered to oversee the execution of the conspirators. While he found it to be somewhat objectionable, he was a man who did his duty, no matter what his own personal feelings might have been.

After the war, Hancock's political aspirations came to the fore when he found himself running for president, opposing Republican James Garfield on the Democratic ticket. Hancock lost, and gave up on the prospect of the White House for good.

Despite developing diabetes, he led a fairly active life, right up until his death in 1886, from a systemic infection. Winfield Scott Hancock left behind a remarkable legacy, as both a superb soldier (to coin a phrase) and an honorable man. I would have given practically anything to sit down and talk with him, something which is, of course, impossible.

Luckily for me, I would be fortunate enough to do the next best thing.

As a young lad growing up in the United Kingdom, I had a long-standing fascination with the American Civil War in general, and with Gettysburg in particular.

Ronald Maxwell's TV movie *Gettysburg*, an adaption of Michael Shaara's Pulitzer Prize-winning novel *The Killer Angels* was (and still is) one of my favorite films. I watched those VHS tapes so often, I practically wore them out. Even now, before I fly out for a trip to Gettysburg, I watch the Blu-Ray the night before.

The cast is uniformly excellent. One of the stand-outs is Brian Mallon, who puts in a stellar turn as Winfield Scott Hancock, a role he would go on to reprise in the prequel, *Gods and Generals.*

In a slightly surreal turn of events, shortly after my stay at the Farnsworth House, I was fortunate enough to obtain an interview with Brian, in which he shared his thoughts regarding both the shoot and the character of Hancock, not to mention a certain tavern on Baltimore Street.

Brian lives in Ireland, and our interview took place on a Sunday afternoon. I was more than a little bit awestruck to begin with, but he soon put me at my ease, and I was delighted to see the old expression that you should never meet your heroes be proven wrong. Brian is a fellow writer, and I very much appreciated him graciously giving up some of his valuable time in order to help me tell this particular story.

"I don't really know much about the Farnsworth House ghost stories, other than the fact that there *are* such stories out there," he said.

"That's okay, Sir—" I replied. He cut me off immediately.

"Don't call me Sir," he chuckled. "'Brian' is fine."

That was going to be a tough habit for me to break. Although he was a thoroughly nice man, I was already a little star-struck. Brian has a very cheerful and friendly voice, but it didn't take a lot of imagination for me to hear the stern, stentorian tones of his character just beneath the surface.

Brian politely asked me about my home and background, making me comfortable in the way that really good interviewees often do. Then discussion turned to the subject of *Gettysburg* or *The Killer Angels,* as it had first been known.

Most actors audition for a role as part of the casting process. Brian's experience on *Gettysburg* was different, and a little unorthodox. Back in the early 1990s, he was running a cafe on Hollywood Boulevard named Cafe Beckett (so called because they used to put on Samuel Beckett plays there). Brian was appearing in an award-winning play titled *Translations.*

One night, director Ron Maxwell was in the audience. He loved the performance, so much so that he came back to the Beckett afterward in order to cast Brian for a role in his upcoming mini-series project. After listening to Brian singing a few Irish songs in the cafe, he asked him to come over to discuss it.

No sooner had the two men sat down to chat than a friend of Brian's happened to wander by. By a strange turn of fate, this gentleman, who was an Apache, happened to be wearing a Civil War-era general's hat. Spotting Brian, he doffed the hat and placed it on top of his friend's head.

The director watched, and suddenly burst out laughing. Brian was puzzled by his reaction; at this point, he still had no idea that he was being considered for the role of a Union general.

Brian tried to give the hat back, but his friend wouldn't hear of it. "You keep it — it suits you!"

"Ron was initially talking about having me play [Sergeant Buster] Kilrain," Brian explained, a role that subsequently went to the actor Kevin Conway. "But he changed his mind fairly quickly on that."

Actors are an unabashedly superstitious breed, particularly those who work in the theater. What were the odds, I wondered, of a man wearing a Civil War general's hat happening to be in the cafe on the same night as the director of an upcoming Civil War production — not only that, but also then placing that hat on Brian's head, and refusing to take it back because it sat so well?

"It almost sounds...*fated,* for lack of a better word," I pointed out.

"Well, it did seem that way to me too," Brian agreed. "I took it as an omen. In fact, I kept that hat. I've still got it somewhere..."

Everybody involved with the production of *Gettysburg* knew that it would be scrutinized endlessly by Civil War aficionados, including the many re-enactors who would help create its vivid battle scenes. Every detail had to be right.

Once he was cast as the great general Winfield Scott Hancock, Brian dove into the minutiae of his subject's life. There was no Internet to consult back then, so he hit the books, studying up on Hancock's career and personality.

"Not just me...everybody did the same. We were given

the names of books to read. The re-enactors know everything about everything, and you wouldn't want to show up there and appear to be ignorant, you know? Sam Elliott [who played Brigadier General John Buford] had hired a researcher for himself, and he gave me a lot of material that he had found about Hancock. That was very useful."

Winfield Scott Hancock was a remarkable man, something of which Brian was very aware, thanks to the reams of research material he had combed through.

"He would have been my favorite character of them all, so I was delighted when I found out that's who I was playing. As I was reading up on him, I liked him. He was a Democrat, so he was glossed over a lot, in terms of the glories, with the Republicans being in office...although despite that, he made enough of a name for himself to run for president."

I mentioned the fact that Hancock had been assigned with overseeing the execution of the Lincoln assassination conspirators, and that he hadn't much liked the task.

"I don't expect that he would," Brian agreed. "Just because of the kind of man that he was. That would not have gone down well with him. He was a very conscientious fellow, well beyond corruption, and always did his duty. He probably would have been a very good president."

Our conversation turned to the subject of the battlefield itself. Just walking the ground at Gettysburg, there is a sense that momentous things happened there.

"Gettysburg was a turning point in the war. So many fellows dead at the end of it — horrible. My mother's side of the family was in America at that time, and my grandmother's uncle, Jimmy Powers, fought in the war (though he wasn't at Gettysburg).

"There is a wonderful aura about Gettysburg," Brian went on. I asked him what it had felt like to be in uniform, riding a horse, at the head of columns of troops, with musketry and cannon fire going off all around him. "That took it to a whole new level. It was an incredible feeling to be out there like that, and in such a position. Of course, the center of the battlefield is so full of monuments, you couldn't possibly film there…we were about a mile and a half up the way, where you had essentially the same land formations.

"I thought we did the story proud. That movie had a wonderful script. It was so accurate — Ron is amazing that way. I was there from day one of the shoot. The Confederates shot their scenes first. We all hung out at the

Farnsworth House. Along with a couple of friends of mine from Ireland — Barry McEvoy and Conn Horgan — who were also on the film, we were called 'the Irish Brigade.' The fella who ran the book shop at the Farnsworth wrote up a piece about it that might be of interest to you."

Brian was referring to a piece called *Killer Angels '92: Campaign Notes from the Farnsworth Tavern*, written by John S. Peterson, a framed copy of which hangs in the tavern to this day. He writes:

Leading the Rebel pack was actor Tom Berenger. In the guise of Gen. James Longstreet, Berenger presented swords to all his officers, and in short order designated the Farnsworth House Tavern as the official "Officers Club" of the First Corps, Army of Northern Virginia. As might be expected, the Tavern soon became the scene of some of the merriest Civil War parties since Jeb Stuart rode rings around McClellan.

Mr. Peterson then goes on to recount actor Stephen Lang, playing the colorful Confederate cavalry general George Pickett, climbing on top of the bar and declaring: "At long last, I've taken the high ground."

According to his account, the actors portraying the Union officers were a little less boisterous when they took over the Farnsworth Tavern after the boys in gray had vacated it. Brian Mallon was there until the very end of shooting, and grew very fond of the historic old house.

"The owners of the Farnsworth just let us have the run of the place. Everybody was so friendly. It was just a great place to be, and a lot of fun. I wasn't too busy for the first few weeks of filming, so I was in there a lot. A good place to get a pint and just watch the world go by, and all in good company."

Brian didn't stay at the Farnsworth, being billeted instead at the equally historic Gettysburg Hotel in the center of town. He came back to Gettysburg for the 25th anniversary of the film, however, and didn't pass up the chance to drop in at one of his favorite old haunts.

"I went back to the Farnsworth last Spring. We got a nice greeting there. It's such a great place. That's where we hung out...our headquarters!"

Blood and Bricks
A Short Story

"Damn, Amos, but it's a going to be a hot one." Charlie Connor wiped the sweat from his brow with the back of one blue-sleeved forearm.

"We've seen worse," Amos said, relaxing just enough to rest his back against a tombstone. The cool stone felt good against the skin of his neck. "And call me Sergeant."

"I didn't mean *that*, Sergeant." If the twenty year-old son of a farmer was annoyed at being corrected, he showed no outward sign of it. He simply nodded up at the merciless sun, bearing down on them from a cloudless blue sky. Then he pointed to the north, well beyond the limits of the cemetery where their regiment, the 154th New York, now bivouacked. "I was talking about *that.*"

The sergeant had to admit that the boy had a point. Taller than Charlie by a good head, Amos had a full beard and the weathered, leathery skin of a man who had spent many a day exposed to the elements. Both the sun and the wind had taken their toll, making him look older than his true age of thirty-three. He looked up from the thing that was cupped in his hands and took in the scene that was playing out both in and around the small town they had spent the past few hours marching toward at the double-time.

Amos had known that there was a fight going on — a *proper* fight, not just some little scrap between regiments of cavalry — long before he set eyes on the town named Gettysburg. What had at first sounded like the distant rumble of thunder had turned out to be something entirely more ominous: the full-throated roar of an artillery duel. When they'd gotten closer, the sound of rifles volleying back and forth had punctuated the cannon fire, letting his seasoned soldier's ear know that the fighting had already gotten down to close range. Infantrymen were slugging it out alongside the artillerists.

"Looks like old Bobby Lee's finally going to stand and put up a fight," Charlie had smirked, marching with the ease of a youngster whose legs didn't ache and grow stiff quite as readily as those of an older man. Amos almost envied him his limber feet and easy stride, one which allowed the boy to eat up the miles with little in the way of complaint.

Oh, to be young again…

It hadn't helped that the infantry, always given short shrift, had been made to march cross-country over the fields, leaving the roads to the wagon trains and the heavy artillery that they supplied.

"Lee's not afraid of a good fight," he cautioned the private. "He proved *that* at Chancellorsville."

Chancellorsville…The boy had joined the regiment after that fight, had never seen a shot fired in anger, but Amos had. He was as brave as the next man, but even the mention of that place made him want to vomit. The fighting had been brutal, even by the standards set by this hellish war, but he had acquitted himself admirably. That was why he now wore sergeant's stripes, after all. They were a tangible reflection of the courage and steadfastness he had shown under fire.

And this…this was shaping up to be even bigger, the sergeant reflected, gazing at the maelstrom now engulfing the town and the land to the north and northwest of it. If he was going to be completely honest, Amos had to admit that the Rebs looked to be giving his brothers-in-arms a hard time of it. Everywhere he looked, the Union lines were in retreat, collapsing inward toward the town itself. Already, irregular clusters of Union soldiers were flooding back through the streets, choking them up in a sea of blue.

Although pockets of resistance were forming here and there, from what he could see, the day was going to belong to the enemy…unless something could be done about it.

Amos craned his neck to look behind him. There was one of the few men who *could* do something about it. General Howard had long since turned his mount over to an adjutant, and now paced back and forth along the crest of the hill, tracing a path in between the gravestones. Every few steps he would stop and raise his binoculars, take in the situation to the north, and utter a few choice cuss words.

Privately, Amos thought such antsy behavior unbecoming of a general. Officers were supposed to look unruffled at all times, especially when things were going bad and their men were there to watch it. Even a sergeant knew *that,* so why didn't they teach them the same thing at West Point?

The sun was still riding high in the sky, but the afternoon was starting to wear on. After they had arrived and made the climb up Cemetery Hill, the men from New York had cleaned their rifles thoroughly and expectantly awaited the call to go the aid of their comrades. Each time a courier galloped up to the general with fresh reports, the men of the 'Hardtack Regiment' had reached for their rifles, anticipating the order to form up and march north into Gettysburg. Their fellow Union soldiers were taking a drubbing down there, while Amos, Charlie, and the other men of Colonel Coster's brigade sat on their behinds and did nothing but watch and wait.

They weren't to be idle for long.

Howard was still staring through his field glasses, his attention riveted to the catastrophe now unfolding before him. Amos returned his attention to the object he held cupped in both hands. He saw Charlie blatantly craning his neck to try and get a look-see, and shuffled his back around to put the gravestone between him and the nosy young lad. He liked Charlie, but the Lord only knew how much of a bother he could be sometimes.

"Come on, Sergeant," Charlie called out, raising his voice to be heard over the sound of cannon fire. "You're always looking at that thing. What is it?"

The tiniest of smiles danced across Amos's lips. "Nothing for you to worry about." He slipped the object of his affection back inside his jacket and returned his attention to the general, who suddenly found himself in conversation with yet another mounted messenger. The officer, a lieutenant, slipped effortlessly from the saddle with the practiced ease of one who had performed the exact same maneuver countless times before. He saluted General Howard, who crisply returned it, then handed over a scrap of paper and waited patiently while the general perused it.

Purely by happenstance, Amos had found himself within earshot of the general earlier on, and had twice heard him reject requests to send troops north to aid in the fight outside Gettysburg. "These men are all that I have — my only reserve!" he had insisted. "Not to mention the fact that they are needed to secure this hill. The enemy will seek to dislodge us from this place by any means possible, and it will take every man we have to hold it against him."

Corps reserve, Amos had thought to himself with more than a little bitterness. *So we sit and we wait, lounging among the gravestones while other men do the fighting and dying.*

Apparently that had now changed, for Howard was beckoning Colonel Coster to come over and join him. Also named Charles, the colonel was only three or four years older than young Charlie, but as the son of a prominent lawyer with a favorable social standing and good political connections, he now found himself in command of an entire brigade. Amos didn't envy him that particular responsibility one whit.

Fully aware that it was considered rude to eavesdrop, the sergeant nonetheless couldn't help himself. Staring out across the rows of tombstones, some of them now chipped and broken, he feigned indifference, while at the same time straining his ears to overhear the conversation between the colonel in charge of his brigade and the commanding general himself.

"General Schurz is sorely pressed, it seems," Howard said, not bothering to lower his voice. "Our line to the north is in danger of being breached. You are directed to take your brigade to bolster it, Colonel. Hold the enemy on the outskirts of town, if you can. Do you understand?"

"Yes, sir," Coster nodded. "We shall depart immediately."

The two men did not exchange salutes. Although the custom was commonplace in the garrison and barracks, it was well-known that doing so on the battlefield was a sure-fire way to mark oneself out for death at the hands of an enemy sniper.

"Away and to your duty, sir," Howard said, turning back to scan the north with his binoculars. Dismissed, Coster began calling for his officers to attend him.

"Up you get, Charlie." Using the tombstone for leverage, Amos got to his feet, picking up his rifle.

All around them, the men of the 154th were following suit. Orders had apparently been issued, because their own regimental commander, Colonel Allen, was coming their way with a determined stride, calling his soldiers to form column of march.

The company commanders and NCOs knew their business, but there was little work for them to do other than to help organize the men into a cohesive marching order. Every single man of the 154th was itching to get down there into the thick of it and help out their hard-pressed comrades.

"Come on boys, keep those lines straight." Colonel Allen prowled up and down the column, casting a critical eye over the winding formation. They had a few minutes to spare. Their fellow New Yorkers of the 134th were taking the lead, with Colonel Coster at their head. Behind the 154th came the remaining two regiments in his brigade, the 27th and 73rd, all fine Pennsylvania boys.

Amos felt like no rebel army ever assembled could stand against them today. A bugler sounded the march. The New Yorkers stepped off smartly. Cemetery Hill angled downward toward the town itself. Once the grass gave way to dirt, the Union soldiers kicked up a cloud of dust that announced their coming.

Beginning to sweat, Amos thought briefly about pulling his canteen and taking a sip of water, but that would have to wait until they stopped. He could feel his collar sticking to his neck, beginning to chafe against the nape. It was an irritant, nothing more, and an almost welcome distraction, keeping his brain from contemplating the fact that they were heading into battle — a battle that some of them would not come back from.

Not him, though. Amos had to believe that, even with men falling on both sides to shot and shell, he would make it out alive. He had too much to live for, his whole entire world waiting for him at home. The thought of never getting back to them just didn't bear thinking about.

He absently stroked his breast pocket, feeling the reassuring presence of what it held — a talisman against all the evils of the world. His reason for marching. His reason for fighting; for *living.*

Dying didn't scare the burly sergeant as much as suffering a horrific injury. He had seen men fall at Chancellorsville, good, strong, and healthy men, their arms and legs mangled by flying lead. Screaming and crying for their mothers in the most undignified fashion, they had been carted off to the butchers, the so-called 'surgeons,' to have the mutilated limbs sawn off. Those who did not die from the utter shock of the barbarous procedures were reduced to being little more than an object of pity.

How was a man supposed to support his family without the use of his arms or legs? No, far better to die quickly and cleanly than to suffer such a cruel and twisted fate.

"The Rebs're comin' and there's thousands of 'em!"

The panicked cry shook Amos from his reverie. He looked up to see who had spoken. They were on the outskirts of town now. The empty slopes of the hill had given way to houses that were scattered sparsely on either side of the column, growing closer together with every passing minute. Gaggles of soldiers in blue were coming toward them from the opposite direction, their faces sweat-streaked with dirt, grime, and in some cases, blood.

One of these soldiers, a heavy-set man, called out like a prophet of doom.

"There's regiments and regiments of them Johnnies comin'! We didn't stand a chance!"

To his disgust, Amos noted that the man carried no weapon.

A soldier without a weapons is about as useful as tits on a bull. He shook his head, fingering the wooden stock of his Enfield rifle. Its solidity was comforting.

Yet Amos couldn't find it within himself to think too badly of these men. For every handful of soldiers that passed him, heading for the rear, came one so grievously wounded that he could not walk or stand. A sergeant from some unknown regiment lay sprawled on his belly, laying motionless in a pool of blood. A red-smeared trail indicated that the man had crawled on his hands and knees for quite a distance before finally collapsing, succumbing to what Amos guessed was a gut wound.

There but for the grace of God...

As they passed through the town square, the throng of blue-coated soldiers fleeing from the enemy began to look less like a retreat and more like a rout. Most refused to look the New Yorkers in the eye, averting their gaze or looking down at their feet rather than acknowledge their defeat.

As the soldiers made their way to the northern fringes of Gettysburg, Amos couldn't help but notice that the spirit of comradeship seemed to be evaporating fast. The advancing Union soldiers were not above shoulder-barging and elbowing them out of the way, having little time for those who broke and ran when things got a little too hot. Now the New Yorkers would have to shoulder their share of the load. From his position close to the front of the column, Amos could see Colonel Allen, just a few steps ahead and off to one side.

The column angled to the right, taking Stratton Street. Mounted on a beautiful, glossy-coated gelding, Colonel Coster reined to a halt alongside Colonel Allen and began to issue orders.

"Sir." Allen inclined his head respectfully.

"Colonel. I have spoken with General Schurz. If these men are to be believed" — Coster gestured toward the flood tide of retreating I and XI Corps men — "then a large force of enemy soldiers is advancing this way, along the Harrisburg Road. We are to stop them at all costs."

"Understood, Sir." Amos watched his commanding officer carefully. The man seemed completely unperturbed by his orders, his face showing no more concern than he would if asked to take a Sunday morning stroll. "How are we to deploy?"

"There is a brick yard up ahead, belonging to a man named Kuhn. The family is long since gone, I am told. You are to deploy there. Your boys will be the center of our line.

They're good men, Charles; *solid* men, fine soldiers, and I know that they will hold. The 134th shall deploy to your right, and the 27th to your left. Three regiments should be more than adequate to hold the line — I would expect nothing less of Pennsylvanians and New Yorkers." A faint smile tugged at his lips. Amos took it for quiet pride, rather than self-effacement.

"We will not let you down, Sir."

"By God, I know you will not." Twisting in his saddle, Coster looked back along the length of the marching column. "I'm to deploy the 73rd in the town square. That will give us a reserve, in the event that things go badly."

"Let us pray that they do not."

"Indeed," Coster agreed fervently. "Now, go on and deploy, if you please. I must see to the rest of my brigade." Pivoting the horse around, the brigade commander trotted away, presumably to deliver those same instructions to the Pennsylvanian regiments who were bringing up the rear.

Up ahead on the eastern side of the street was what had to be the brickyard. The 134th passed through a gateway alongside a two-story house, peeling off smartly to the right. Following right on their heels, Colonel Allen led his own New Yorkers straight ahead. Amos could see three brick structures that looked like kilns standing off to the right, in front of a slow-running creek. Beyond that, on the north and east sides, were a series of wheat fields.

"Have the men form lines — smartly, now!" Allen ordered. The junior officers and NCOs hustled the enlisted men into ranks. The colonel stood motionless, appraising his position with a critical eye. Finally, he indicated a series of post-and-rail fences that bordered the wheat fields. Drawing his sword, he used it for emphasis, sweeping the blade along the direction of the fence-line. "I want the lines deployed along those fences. The enemy will have to hit us from the north and east."

Off to their right, Lt. Colonel Jackson, the commanding officer of the 134th, apparently had the exact same idea. His men were forming parallel lines behind the wooden fences, the barrels of their weapons resting upon the rails. The ground sloped down toward the creek, meaning that the men on the right were lower than the 154th, and the Pennsylvanians to their left were higher up. It was a hell of a strange place to fight an engagement.

"This is it, Amos!" Charlie's voice was full of excitement. "The Rebs are really coming!"

"That's *Sergeant*," Amos replied absently, moving forward and chivvying the younger man along with his free hand. When they reached a likely spot along the fence-line, Amos took a knee and grabbed a fistful of Charlie's collar. Pulling him in close, he said, "Now you listen to me, Charlie, and you listen good. This is your first fight. Whatever you think it's going to be like, you're *wrong*."

"But—"

"Just shut up and *listen* a minute. I've seen men piss their pants at the first sign of the enemy. Bigger men than you. I've seen 'em shot down and crying out for their mommas because they couldn't get up and walk. Whatever you think this is going to be like, Charlie, it *ain't*. So you stick close to me, a'right? You stay *right here* at my hip, and don't move. Just think about that rifle in your hands and the man you're pointing it at. Breathe slow. Aim small. Miss small. Got it?"

"Yes, sir."

"Not 'sir.' *Sergeant*."

"Yes, *Sergeant*." Amos's impromptu speech had taken some of the wind out of the boy's sails, which had been precisely the point. All he knew of war up until now had been stories. That was all about to change. Charlie was about to get his first proper look at the beast, and Amos wanted him — wanted them *both* — to survive it.

Off to their left, just past the fence was the Harrisburg Road. It looked wide enough to be one of the main routes in and out of town, which meant that the Rebs would probably use it as a main axis of their advance. The 27th Pennsylvania had that covered, its men strung out in a double line along the fence. As for the rest, well…he eyed the ground in front of him, sloping gently uphill, row after row of tall, golden corn stalks. They shone in the sunlight, drifting lazily from side to side in the slight breeze…

No.

Some of the motion was unnatural. Slowly, figures began to appear, smashing down the stalks. Uncased colors, Rebel flags, came toward them, bobbing above a long gray line that grew broader and better-defined with every passing second.

The enemy were here.

"154th — *KNEEL!*"

Amos recognized the voice as being that of the Colonel. On either side of them, those few men who were still standing now sunk down onto one knee, bringing their rifles up into their shoulders and sighting in on the approaching

Confederates.

A man several places off to the left fired. The harsh crack split the still afternoon air. Amos squinted, but did not see any of the oncoming soldiers fall.

"Hold your fire!" roared Colonel Allen. "Steady, lads — not yet. Not. Yet."

The sound of fifes and drums drifted across from the wheat field, a jaunty cadence that somehow managed to seem more ominous than inspirational. Amos felt something twist in his gut, a cold, reptilian thing that slithered around his insides. His mouth suddenly felt bone dry. Was there time for a swig of water? No. He discounted the possibility immediately. The enemy were getting closer. Sunlight glinted from the blades held aloft by their officers. One man twirled his sword lazily above his head, the steel catching the light just so.

Three regiments. We have three regiments, Amos thought to himself, trying to dispel the sickness threatening to take over his belly. *That's nine hundred men. We can withstand anything the Rebs throw at us with nearly a thousand men...*

...can't we?

"Steady...steady..."Allen was standing some twenty

feet behind his own front lines. Amos chanced a quick look back at the colonel, and could hardly credit what he saw. The colonel was as cool as a cucumber, pacing slowly up and down the 154th's line. He had returned his sword to its scabbard and now clasped his hands calmly behind his back, looking for all the world as though he was on a parade ground, preparing to inspect the troops, rather than within spitting distance of an enemy attack.

Coster appeared at his side, equally calm and unruffled. "Remember, 154th, you're shooting uphill," he called out, "so aim low. Ready. Pre-*sent*."

The command to present arms was moot; each man had already sighted in on the oncoming mass of Confederates.

A high, piercing yell suddenly rose from the Confederate ranks, an ululating war-cry calculated to strike fear into the hearts of their enemies and raise courage for the coming charge. Every man in blue knew its name: the Rebel Yell.

The gray ranks charged.

"Fire!"

The entire Union line disappeared in a wall of smoke as hundreds of trigger fingers all squeezed at once, flensing the Rebel formation with a storm of lead balls. For their part, the Union men had no opportunity to see the damage they had wrought. Not only were they too busy ramming home fresh balls into the muzzle of their rifles, but a haze of foul, sulfurous-smelling smoke rendered them effectively blind.

The screams, however, spoke for themselves. At sixty yards, the rifled Enfields shot both straight and true, punching through the flesh of their targets to rupture organs and shatter bone. Confederate soldiers fell en masse, tripping those who ran along behind them.

Amos took comfort in the familiar routine of re-loading his weapon, vigorously shoving the ball deep into the Enfield's barrel with the ramrod. From the corner of his eye, he could see Charlie doing the same thing, though his hands were shaking as he did so.

A thunderous booming noise came from somewhere behind him. The familiar sound came as sweet relief. Artillery. *Friendly* artillery, at that. Somehow, Colonel Coster had managed to get some guns up, Lord bless him. Amos swiped a sleeve across his forehead, trying to keep the sweat-matted hair out of his eyes. Clutching the ramrod tightly in the fingers of his left hand, he pulled the rifle's stock into his shoulder again and pointed the weapon into the still-drifting haze.

The smoke suddenly lit up with hundreds of sparkling

flashes of light, accompanied by the roar of massed gunfire. Now the shoe was on the other foot. Minie balls smacked into the fence behind which Amos and his comrades had taken cover. It was the Bluecoats' turn to suffer. A man two spots to Amos's left fell onto his back, both hands clutching at his face. His black beard was suddenly crimson. Blood spurted from between the soldier's fingers, yet he made not a sound as he writhed on the ground, boots kicking desperately at the fence posts.

"Fire!"

Amos couldn't tell which colonel had issued the command, and neither did he care. He pulled the trigger, firing blindly into the smoky miasma, thickening it even more. Was that a scream? He wasn't sure. More flashes from directly in front. Something whipped past his left air, whining like an angry hornet.

A grunt came from somewhere behind him, followed by the sound of a man falling in the second rank. Amos didn't turn to see who had been hit, didn't dare. He fumbled inside his cartridge box, fingers desperately seeking more ammunition. His hands were sweaty, almost making him drop the ramrod, but somehow he managed to drop a third ball into the rifle's muzzle and began tamping it down.

More gunfire came from beyond the fence. Murky shapes were slowly bleeding into view. What he at first took to be a mountain swaying from side to side finally resolved into an enemy battle flag when a gust of wind exposed a clear patch in the smoke. It couldn't have been more than fifty yards away, by his estimation.

Figuring that he could hit the color bearer at that close range, Amos sighted in on where he thought the base of the staff must be and pulled the trigger. The rifle bucked, slamming hard into his shoulder, and he was rewarded with the sight of the flag sliding slowly down and backward out of sight.

Take that, Johnny Reb!

He could hear the fire intensifying off to the right. The 134th were giving the enemy hell.

"I got me one, Amos!" Charlie yelled, his face a grinning mask of adrenaline-fueled excitement. "Think he were an officer, too. Saw him fall!"

"Quit your hollerin' and reload," snapped Amos, not bothering to correct the boy this time. There was a time and a place for etiquette, and this wasn't it. "There's plenty more Rebs out there for you to shoot."

Nodding excitedly, Charlie went for another ball. The

enemy was closer now, individual faces visible through gaps in the smoke. Amos took his own order to heart and began reloading for the fourth time.

They're mighty close. Why has nobody told us to fix bayonets?

Raising the rifle to his shoulder, Amos sent another ball into the smoke. His hands were working without conscious thought now, smoothly and independently running through the reloading sequence that had been drummed into him on countless drill grounds and on more than one battlefield.

From somewhere off to the right, there came a colossal roar. Without breaking his flow, Amos glanced that way. What he saw horrified him. The men of the 134th were getting to their feet, turning around, and…retreating?

"Hold the line!" somebody bellowed from behind them. "Hold the line, boys, for pity's sake!"

But it was to no avail. The New Yorkers were being overrun. The ground behind their portion of the fence was strewn with their dead and wounded. Many of those who turned to run were shot down. Now the Rebels were at the fence, clambering over it.

Amos swung his rifle around and put a bullet into a Confederate officer, just as he was straddling the fence rail.

The man's head snapped backward. His black felt hat flew away in a blossoming red mist. The dead officer's body flopped backward into the ranks of the men he had been leading, disappearing from sight on the other side of the fence.

"We're being flanked!" a man's voice screamed hoarsely. "Get the hell out of here!"

"Amos…should we run?" Fear was written all over Charlie's face now, every last trace of the ebullience he had shown just moments ago now wiped away at the sight of the 134th's plight. Not all of the Union soldiers were running. Some still stood their ground. They didn't stand a chance. The onrushing tide of Confederates engulfed them, shooting them down where they knelt and crouched.

Amos opened his mouth to speak, to tell the boy that no, they were not going to retreat; they were going to hold fast and wait for the colonel to send them support. There was a reserve back in the town square, he wanted to say, but he recognized the folly of that idea before he ever gave it voice. The right of the line was collapsing. By the time the 73rd could get here, they would all be dead.

Somebody punched him, harder than he had ever been hit in his life. Unbidden, Amos's hand flew up to his breast.

Fortunately, the precious contents of that inner pocket were still safe. He could feel them there, his heart, safe and sound.

And warm.

"Sergeant...you've been hit," Charlie said, his voice suddenly small and frightened. Amos looked down. His blue jacket was slowly darkening as a red stain spread across it, expanding from a perfectly round hole in the fabric.

At first, there was no pain — and then there was, a sudden flux of agony that took his breath away. Amos tried to breathe. The pain flared so intensely that he almost passed out. He tried to stand but instead fell backward onto his buttocks, all of the strength gone from his legs.

A Confederate soldier mounted the fence, using one hand for purchase and holding his rifle with the other. He paused, one foot on the top rail of the fence, and swung the weapon to bear on Amos. The flash-bang startled them both. Charlie shot the man in the belly, folding him in half at the waist. The falling Confederate took two of his comrades with him as he went down, buying Charlie a precious few seconds to do what had to be done.

Slinging the rifle over his shoulder by its strap, the boy got his hands under Amos's armpits and began to drag him backwards, away from the firing line. On either side, soldiers of the 154th traded shots with their attackers, unwilling to give up their defensive position no matter what. Most had seen their brother New Yorkers shot down from behind when they had tried to flee, and weren't about to let the same thing happen to them. Some were fixing bayonets, getting ready for the grim and bloody business of hand-to-hand combat.

"I'll get you out of here, Sergeant," Charlie panted. "You just hang on." He dug in with his heels, gritting his teeth at the effort of moving the bigger man's weight. Amos tried to kick with his legs in order to add a little impetus, but he was starting to lose sensation in his feet.

"Getting…real hard…to breathe." Amos was suddenly tired, so very tired. He wanted to ask the boy to let him down for a minute so that he could close his eyes. Just a minute or two. No longer. Just enough for him to get his strength back.

Amos's head began to loll. He looked to the left, where the Pennsylvanians were holding their section of the line. Gray-jacketed troops were across the fence, overwhelming the outnumbered defenders in a brutal melee. On the northern edge, more Confederate troops were sweeping around to flank the Union position.

How had things gone bad so quickly? Amos couldn't

fathom it. Worse still, he was starting not to care. He felt as if he was floating through the blue sky without a care in the world, unconcerned by the screams of the dead and the dying, the harsh crack of the rifle and boom of the cannon.

None of it mattered any more. All that mattered was getting home.

Home to them.

He reached into his jacket and pulled out that most precious of things. Clutching it with his fingers, he tried to look on it one last time, but his eyes stubbornly refused to focus.

Amos felt cold. So very cold.

"Hang on, Sergeant Humiston, okay? Just you hang on for a little longer!" Somehow, incredibly, they had made it out into the street once more. Although bullets whined all around them, the intensity of the gunfire was much slacker than it had been on the firing line where Amos had been hit.

Charlie was sweating heavily, salty droplets falling from his nose and forehead to spatter on Amos's upturned face. Amos didn't care. All he cared about was THEM. "Hang on, Sergeant! Just you hang on! Just you hang—"

The boy never saw the bullet that took his life. The Minie Ball tore through his throat, severing an artery.

Charlie fell into the street, knocking himself unconscious on the hard stone. It took less than a few heartbeats for him to drown in his own blood.

Amos swatted at him impotently, wanting to help the boy, but at the same time knowing that he was beyond all help now but that of the Lord. Nor was Amos in any fit state to be His agent. His breath came in fast, ragged gasps, each one bringing fresh pain. He tried to crawl as best he could, but barely made it more than a few feet before his arms stopped working properly.

Tears began to roll down his cheek, tears of impotence, frustration, and above all, rage — a rage born of the knowledge that he had lost them.

Amos was dying. He knew it, deep down, with absolute certainty. All he wanted to do was look upon their faces for the last time. Just one last time. He could feel the photograph clutched within his fist, locked in a death grip, but try as he might, he just could not bring his hand up to his face.

It wasn't even close to sunset yet, but the world was somehow turning dark.

"Phylinda," he croaked, wanting to die with their names upon his lips. "Franklin.

"Frederick.

"Alice."

His eyes couldn't see any more, so he closed them. His mind's eye still worked, however, and their faces suddenly sprang unbidden into his mind, full of light and joy, just as they had appeared when they had waved him good-bye.

Amos felt so, so weary, and decided that now was a good time to give himself permission to rest. Just for a little while. As he drifted away, four faces — three of them adorable young children, and the fourth the great love of his life — accompanied him down into the darkness.

He never let the photograph go.

AUTHOR'S NOTE

Many tragic human interest stories arose from the battle of Gettysburg, yet none captured the public imagination on a similar scale to that of Sergeant Amos Humiston, Company C, 154th New York Volunteer Infantry.

It is a difficult and, some might say, presumptious (if not arrogant) thing indeed to ascribe words and emotions to a flesh-and-blood man such as Amos Humiston, a devoted family man who really did walk the earth. This is a work of fiction, and SHORT fiction at that; its intent is to move the reader, not to provide a definitive account of one brave man's life and death. I wanted to write about the last hours of Amos's life because I found them deeply moving, whenever I encountered his story in the history books and TV/movie dramatizations.

He was a brave man, and died the death of a brave man. I hope that his portrayal in this story does the man justice, inasmuch as it possibly can.

Amos did indeed die in the fierce fighting at John Kuhn's Brickyard, and the events of the fierce but bloody conflict did happen pretty much as the story describes them. The characters who appear are also real, with the exception of young Charlie, who is a product of the author's imagination.

The 900 men of Colonel Coster's brigade were basically fed into a meat grinder at John Kuhn's brick yard, outnumbered as they were by a vastly superior Confederate force of two brigades that brought a little under 3,000 men to bear on them. Even the support given by a battery of four Napoleon cannons didn't tip the odds in Coster's favor. The Confederates simply extended their line at both ends and enveloped the weaker Union force, rolling up each flank and cutting off their already limited routes of escape.

Although hindsight is always 20/20, it does seem obvious that putting a brigade-sized unit in such a position with both flanks unsupported was asking for trouble. Yet looking at it from Coster's point of view, his orders left him little choice but to try and delay the Confederate advance long enough for the broken remains of the retreating Union Corps' to attain the safety of friendly lines once more.

What little time this engagement ultimately bought came at a terrible cost — an entire Union brigade was sacrificed.

The 134th were indeed the first to retreat, as described, ordered to do so by their commanding officer. It is difficult to blame Lt. Col. Jackson for this, as his regiment had already sustained heavy losses from enemy fire and was now being encircled and destroyed in details. It is also true that many more of his men were killed when they attempted to withdraw. For turning their back on the attacking Confederates, they paid the ultimate price.

Positioned on his brigade's left with the Pennsylvanians, Coster retreated when that flank showed signs of buckling too. That just left the 154th, and as the old saying goes, "the center could not hold." Allen wisely gave the order for his surviving men to withdraw in the general direction of the gatehouse and North Stratton Street. Some of his men actually made it that far, dispersing into the streets of Gettysburg and trying to find hiding places. Some hid in the cellar of the Kuhn house itself, and were soon found and captured, but others had more success, hiding with some of the town's residents. Lt. Col. Jackson of the 134th actually had to don a disguise in order to make it back to friendly lines.

Contemporary accounts tell us that the men of the 154th New York got off no more than six to nine shots apiece in the brickyard before being totally overwhelmed by the enemy. Although Colonel Allen and two other officers escaped with their lives, the vast majority of the men from

Coster's brigade were captured en masse or killed, along with two of the supporting artillery pieces.

Today, a mural depicting the valor of those who fought at Kuhn's Brickyard can be found and admired at the site itself. The artist is Mark H. Dunkelman, who also chronicled the history of the 154th New York, and has written an excellent account of the battle (and its immortalization in paint) titled *"Gettysburg's Coster Avenue: The Brickyard Fight: and the Mural."*

Mr. Dunkelman's book is an outstanding resource for those seeking to understand this oft-overlooked engagement, and I cannot recommend it highly enough. It provided an excellent source during the writing of this piece of fiction, though I must stress that any factual errors to be found in this tale are strictly my own.

The possession which Amos prized so dearly was, of course, a photograph of his three children. When his body was discovered after the battle, his identity was unknown. This prompted a national search for the children depicted in the image, which ultimately led to the discovery of his widow, Phylinda Humiston, and their three children back in Portville, New York. Phylinda now knew for certain why she had not head anything further from her husband after the

Battle of Gettysburg.

Amos Humiston is buried in the Gettysburg National Cemetery, on the hallowed ground which he and so many of his brothers-in-arms fought to preserve.

Acknowledgments

To the reader: Thank you for spending your hard-earned money and valuable time in order to read this book. It is my sincere hope that you have enjoyed it, and would ask you to please consider rating the book at the website it was purchased or borrowed from. In the current writing market, books tend to live and die by their reviews and ratings; your time would therefore be greatly appreciated.

Some other thanks are due to the people without whom this book would not have been possible.

Laura, for her support throughout the research and writing process.

Jason and Anna, for living the adventure with me.

Mr. and Mrs. Schulz, owners of the Farnsworth House, for keeping this beautiful place open and offering such a warm and friendly welcome.

Kayla Russell, storyteller extraordinaire, and her fellow storytellers at the Farnsworth House, who are working to keep its fascinating history alive for others to enjoy.

Pam Barry, Steve Barry, and Erik Julian at the Gettysburg Battlefield Bash, for inviting me back, constantly supporting my work, and being generally awesome. I am very fortunate to call you all my friends.

Anthony and Deena Holmes, Rob and Michelle Natalini, Lisa, Nikki, and Chenita, for sharing your experiences in two very haunted rooms.

Nicole Novelle and Rob Szarek, for sharing that haunted attic with me – and for good companionship.

Vivian Vega, for talking frankly about her haunted experiences at the Farnsworth House.

Last, but by no means least, General Hancock himself: Brian Mallon, who is every bit as superb as his namesake.

Thank you all from the bottom of my heart — RE

By The Same Author

Haunted Longmont
In Search of the Paranormal
The World's Most Haunted Hospitals
The Haunting of Asylum 49 (with Cami Andersen)
Spirits of the Cage (with Vanessa Mitchell)
Visiting the Ghost Ward
Trail of Terror
Haunted Healthcare
Haunted Healthcare 2
Colorado UFOs
The Dead Below: The Haunting of Denver Botanic Gardens
The Fairfield Haunting: On the Gettysburg Ghost Trail
The Horrors of Fox Hollow Farm